"Each of us must decide whether we will live [up to] our God-given potential. The reality is, most [...] rather, most people make God out to be too sm[...] Steve Smothermon elevates the greatness of who God is and wh[...] to do in our life. He shows us how to live up to our faith instead of down to our fears."—**Gerald Brooks**, Grace Outreach Center, Plano, Texas, author of *Understanding Your Pain Threshold*

"Steve Smothermon has written his finest work yet out of the research laboratory of his own big problems, only to discover that God is bigger. This is not only a book of hope but a roadmap to solutions, which makes it a book of help!"—**Bishop Dale C. Bronner**, DMin, author and pastor, Word of Faith Family Worship Cathedral, Atlanta, Georgia

"Pastor Steve Smothermon is a no-nonsense kind of guy. I've never known him to sugarcoat a sermon or a bit of advice he gives to a parishioner. He takes complex issues and makes them easy to understand, giving real answers to real problems. If you have a problem that is troubling your heart, mind, or body, *Big Problems, Bigger God* is your book!"—**Willie George**, founding pastor, Church on the Move, Tulsa, Oklahoma

"In *Big Problems, Bigger God,* Steve Smothermon takes us on a journey to discover that the circumstances we face are only a small part of the problem; the true nature of the conflict is defined by our responses to setbacks. Steve's straightforward, practical advice teaches us how to allow God to pave our paths with the very complications that would otherwise become stumbling blocks. I dare you to take this journey and discover how letting go of circumstantial helplessness can lead to a life of joy-filled purposefulness—not just in spite of the problems that come your way, but perhaps even *because* of them."—**Tommy Barnett**, pastor, Phoenix First and founder, Phoenix and Los Angeles Dream Centers

"There's an old Christian song that begins, 'Got any rivers you think are uncrossable? Got any mountains you can't tunnel through?' Who hasn't faced a tough situation in life? If you're going through a trial, Steve Smothermon offers practical insights that will renew your mind and inspire you to put your hope in someone who has a name: Jesus. Don't stay stuck—God is truly bigger than your problem!"—**James Robison**, founder and president, LIFE Outreach International, founder and publisher, The Stream (stream.org)

"Steve Smothermon has a timely message that will empower and encourage you. Inside these pages, he realigns perspective to a vantage point on the edge of the very hands of God, where the truth becomes refreshingly visible that each life is infused with God-given potential to overcome any adversity, to accomplish above and beyond all that we can ask or imagine, and to become all that God has long before planned for us to be in Christ."—**Carl Toti**, pastor, Trinity Church, Lubbock, Texas

"Steve Smothermon doesn't mince words in *Big Problems, Bigger God.* Written from a place of honest reflection of his own frustrations, Steve's thought-provoking ideas are full of encouraging hope that begins to heal and release the pains of your past. He then lays out a clear set of principles to overcome injustices and intimidating circumstances. Without a doubt, his book will help you become the best you that God made you to be."—**Rick Bezet**, lead pastor, New Life Church of Arkansas

"This is a remarkable book that explains in practical terms and examples how the dynamics of changing your thinking will impact your life. Steve Smothermon will challenge and educate you to get more out of life by adjusting the filter you look through. *Big Problems, Bigger God* shows how our beliefs, actions, and decisions affect our success. I loved the way Steve took specific examples from his own life and the lives of many great people to create a process to help us all change for the better. Do yourself a favor and read this treasure of truth. This book is truly an investment in your future and the lives of the people you touch."—**Sanford G. Kulkin**, PhD, founder/CEO, PeopleKeys

"In *Big Problems, Bigger God,* Steve Smothermon explains the key to overcoming adversity and growing in your faith so that you can reach new heights in your walk with God. We all encounter setbacks in life, but how we respond to those setbacks and apply the lessons we learn is what defines us as a person. Through sound biblical principles and detailed personal experience, Steve takes the reader on a journey of discovery, showing the glory of God at work in all things. This book is a wakeup call to the body of Christ, and I recommend it to anyone looking for a fresh perspective and a new direction in their lives."—**Matthew Barnett**, senior pastor, Angelus Temple and cofounder of The Dream Center

BIG PROBLEMS, BIGGER GOD

STEVE SMOTHERMON

HARVEST HOUSE PUBLISHERS
EUGENE, OREGON

Cover by Dugan Design Group, Bloomington, Minnesota

Cover illustration © Dugan Design Group

Published in association with the literary agency of The FEDD Agency, Inc., PO Box 341973, Austin, TX 78734.

BIG PROBLEMS, BIGGER GOD

Published by Harvest House Publishers
Eugene, Oregon 97402
www.harvesthousepublishers.com

Library of Congress Cataloging-in-Publication Data
    Smothermon, Steve, 1967-
    Big problems, bigger God / Steve Smothermon.
        pages cm
    ISBN 978-0-7369-6392-3 (pbk.)
    ISBN 978-0-7369-6393-0 (eBook)
    1. Christian life. I. Title.
    BV4501.3.S65743 2015
    248.8'6—dc23
                                                2015002119

Printed in the United States of America

15 16 17 18 19 20 21 22 23 / BP-JH / 10 9 8 7 6 5 4 3 2 1

This book is dedicated to my wife, Cynthia,
who has loved me unconditionally—
and to all those who have the courage
to overcome whatever obstacles life throws their way.

ACKNOWLEDGMENTS

To all those who call Legacy Church their home, it is a real pleasure to serve you each day.

I've enjoyed collaborating with Bill Blankschaen on this book. Without his writing talent, it would not have been possible.

Thank you to Esther Fedorkevich, a truly talented agent, for being willing to work with me to get this project published.

A big thanks to Denise for her input and to Grant for his diligence in deciphering my handwriting.

To Terry Glaspey at Harvest House Publishers, thank you for taking a chance. You and your team have been a joy to work with.

And a special thanks to Brooke, Steve, and Kristin. You mean everything to me.

CONTENTS

FOREWORD

From daily annoyances to soul-shattering tragedies and everything in between, it is easy to feel overwhelmed by life's problems. Whether these circumstances are of our own doing or the
result of something out of our control, the right perspective can turn
an annoyance into the anointed and a tragedy into a triumph. Too
often we fall victim to the consequences of our failings, or to the
failings of people and things around us, but when approached in
the right way, problems can define the goal and shape the solution.

In *Big Problems, Bigger God,* Steve Smothermon takes us on a
journey to discover that the circumstances we face are only a small
part of the problem; the true nature of the conflict is defined by
our responses to setbacks. Steve's straightforward, practical advice
teaches us how to allow God to pave our paths with the very complications that would otherwise become stumbling blocks.

The journey won't be easy. You will be asked some difficult questions and challenged to examine your perspectives and attitudes
from the inside out. Steve will encourage you to think beyond your
situation and to re-create the portrait of your life by trusting in
the One who works all things together for your good. Steve will
show you how to go beyond the superficial by tapping into the

supernatural hope that can be accessed only through God's faithfulness and mercy. You will be handed a new lens, and then asked to use it in analyzing how you respond to life's hiccups.

Do you hide and blame, as Adam and Eve did in the garden, or do you step out of the brush and face your problems with a renewed sense of humility and awareness? Do you merely agree with God's Word, content to sit in the boat at the mercy of the storm, or do you wholeheartedly believe in the One who calmed the storm, eager to step out onto the waves with Him?

Pastor Steve pastors a phenomenal church of thousands in Albuquerque, New Mexico. He is a man of great humility, is generous to the core, and a leader among leaders. While he is a hard hitter, his love for people has made him an irresistible leader and personality.

I dare you to take this journey and discover how letting go of circumstantial helplessness can lead to a life of joy-filled purposefulness—not just in spite of the problems that come your way, but perhaps even *because* of them.

Tommy Barnett

Pastor, Phoenix First

Founder, Phoenix and Los Angeles Dream Centers

Part 1

YOUR HOPE
FOR A BETTER LIFE

1

TO EVERYONE
WHO HAS PROBLEMS

When Apollo 13 launched into outer space on Saturday, April 11, 1970, no one expected trouble. Two days later, the mission was still going smoothly. Mission Control in Houston, Texas, even said they were bored. Jack Swigert, Fred Haise, and James Lovell were about to become only the third team of men to land on the moon.

You may be familiar with the rest of the story from the 1995 movie *Apollo 13* starring Tom Hanks and Ed Harris. The crew had just concluded a TV broadcast by wishing the world "a nice evening" when the mission took an unexpected turn. James Lovell describes what happened next:

> Oxygen tank No. 2 blew up, causing No. 1 tank also to fail. We came to the slow conclusion that our normal supply of electricity, light, and water was lost, and we were about 200,000 miles from Earth. We did not even have power to gimbal the engine so we could begin an immediate return to Earth.[1]

Drifting in space, the cabin temperature quickly dropped to a frigid 38° F. Deadly carbon dioxide began building up. Warning lights flashed everywhere. The instruments said that one oxygen tank was empty, and the other was being depleted. As the astronauts looked out the window, they could see precious air leaking from their one remaining oxygen tank.

A moon landing was out of the question. Now they were struggling simply to survive. As they watched the air tank's pressure decrease, they realized they'd soon be completely out of oxygen. And when their last fuel cell died, they'd be out of options. The ship would just skip off the atmosphere and into space—or entomb the three men in a perpetual orbit around the Earth. It's no wonder that Jack Swigert radioed Mission Control with these now famous words: "Houston, we've had a problem."

Where Has All the Hope Gone?

I'm guessing you've never been stranded in outer space with no air and few options for survival. Maybe I'm wrong about that and you've got a really great story to tell. But one thing I do know for sure—you have problems. We all do. Sometimes life can seem like nothing but problems. So I don't need to know the details about your life right now to know that, if your life is at all like mine, you've faced some tough stuff before.

That tough stuff might even be staring you in the face right now. Maybe a friendship has imploded, a marriage has disintegrated, or someone you trusted has betrayed you and you feel an ache within that defies description. Perhaps a disease has painfully restricted your lifestyle, a diagnosis has cut your retirement plans short, or your home has recently been visited by death. Maybe the job you thought was safe and secure just turned into an unexpected pink slip, and your plans for a brighter tomorrow seem to have skipped town.

Or you can't find a job in the first place. In fact, it's been awhile since you dared to look.

Whatever your problem or pain may be, however you might describe the problems your facing, I get it. I've had to face some problems of my own. Some of them happened to me and some were caused by my own mistakes. I'll share more about them later. But I know from experience that it's easy to think that you're alone when facing problems that seem too big for you to handle. I know it's easy to think you're the first to experience anything like what you're facing. But problems are nothing new. Pain and suffering have been with us since Eden. Disappointment has given poets and songwriters plenty of material for thousands of years. There's a reason that the most popular country songs are all about hurts and heartaches. We've all got 'em. We're not the first people for whom life hasn't turned out the way we wanted.

So then why does it feel as if now is different? Why does it feel as if problems are dominating the headlines of our lives and of our culture in general? Why does it seem that so many of us have quit trying to live triumphantly and have settled for drifting aimlessly, as if we no longer had any hope for living a better life?

So many of us seem to agree with the anonymous critic: *Life's tough. Then you die.* Even if we don't say that, we live like we believe it. We live to escape from life. We live for the weekend, for vacation, for the next high—we live waiting for someone else to do something to fix our problems. And if they don't, we get angry.

Maybe it's just me seeing this, but I don't think so. As a pastor of thousands of wonderful people, it's my privilege to interact with a lot of people both close to home here in New Mexico and all over the country. I've noticed a disturbing trend: hope is hard to find. Over the last few years depression has become a worldwide epidemic with 5 percent of the global population suffering from it, according to the World Health Organization. Yet here in the United States, in what may be the most prosperous culture in human history, the situation is even worse. The Centers for Disease Control (CDC) says that almost 10 percent of people in the US from all walks of life suffer from depression. One of the leading indicators? Hopelessness.[2]

What I have discovered over many years of pastoring is that depression is a person's frustration and anger—toward self, others, or society—turned inward in a way that is highly destructive physically, emotionally, and spiritually. We see the ultimate physical destruction when it leads to the tragic choice of suicide. People who commit suicide often do it because they believe there is no other way out of their life, others around them would be better off, or they want to get back at someone else. According to the CDC, suicide was the tenth leading cause of death in the United States in 2011 (the most recent year for such records) with someone dying at his or her own hands every 13.3 minutes. The highest suicide rate (18.6 out of every 100,000 people) is among those in the age bracket between forty-five and sixty-four. The second highest rate (16.9 out of every 100,000) occurred in those eighty-five and older.[3] Tragically, those who have experienced the most of life appear to be most dissatisfied with it, as if their problems just reached a place where they couldn't face them anymore.

Have you felt that same thing? *How can I ever make it with the problems I'm facing? Is there really anything better? Can I really get there from here?* Maybe with the pain you're feeling right now, you're just not that sure anymore. Maybe you've already tried and failed, so you think there's no hope. But I believe that we were not made to face these problems alone. I believe there's a place in us that only God can fill, that nothing else can satisfy. So the solution to our problems is not to look within ourselves but to look up to the One who offers us whatever we need for whatever we face.

Real Hope for the Real World

As the senior pastor of Legacy Church in Albuquerque, it is my privilege to see people overcome problems and live a better life every day through faith in the God who is bigger than the problems they face. By following God's wisdom that He's given us in the Bible, they find hope. And I don't mean just hope for the life beyond this one, but in the rough-and-tumble world of the here and now.

I met a lady through our ministry to the homeless who demonstrated how God's wisdom changes our outlook. After someone on our Dream Team (what we call our awesome ministry volunteers) gave her a Bible, she became fascinated with God's Word. Although she still lived on the streets, she started believing God's promises and thanking Him for the few things she did have. After she learned of God's call to work as we are able (2 Thessalonians 3:10), she readily accepted when another lady in our church offered to pay her to do some odd jobs around her house. It was the first time she had worked at all in five years. She then learned of God's call to tithe and give generously (Proverbs 3:9-10). So after being paid, she put 10 percent of her earnings in one of our giving envelopes and dropped it in the offering bucket during a Wednesday night service. As she described it then, one of the greatest feelings she had ever felt was showing honor to God as her Provider with that offering. Before long, she had found a great job and rented a house that she later purchased—a first-time home buyer at age forty-three. And it all started with trusting God's wisdom for living a better life.

Your version of a better life will likely look different from hers. It may be the ability to show up to a steady job and put food on the table for your family. Maybe it means finding freedom from an addiction that's enslaved you for years. A better life for another person may be seeing a shattered relationship restored by the power and grace of God. For others, it could look like having material blessing and influence to spread a message of hope in Christ to needy people groups around the world.

You may not even have a clear sense of what your better life could be; you just know you've got problems. That's OK. Your life is different from everyone else's life. Some people might not find my friend's transition from homelessness to a house of her own to be all that impressive, but for her that better life was unthinkable just a short time ago. When we follow God's wisdom, He turns the unimaginable into our new reality. No matter how big your problems may be, here's one thing I know: God is bigger.

God's Best for You

Everything I'm about to share with you is not theoretical, pie-in-the-sky stuff, but proven, practical truths. It doesn't come from dusty theological books, but from the journey of my life lived out in the light of God's Word. I've had to learn the hard way how to overcome problems or stuff I perceived to be problems. I've learned to change my thinking by being real and recognizing God at work in my life, seeing how He truly teaches and guides me. As the Author and Finisher of my journey, God has taught and guided my steps—even during those times when I was too hard-headed to listen. And there were lots of those times, let me tell you.

I've learned that my responsibility is not to fix all my problems myself, but to follow the One who gives true peace in the face of any problem. Jesus said, "I have told you these things, so that in me you may have peace. In this world you will have trouble. But take heart! I have overcome the world" (John 16:33). If I am willing to be honest about my shortcomings, I can find peace as I grow and mature in my relationship with God.

Now don't get me wrong, as my wife will be happy to tell you, I am still a work in progress. But I'm more willing now to hold up my thoughts next to the Bible to make sure they line up with God's thoughts and His best for me. And when I do that, my perspective shifts. Suddenly the problems I face, as real and as painful as they may be, don't seem as big as they did before. And that's where hope comes from.

But if we have no hope, where does that leave us? I don't know about you, but if there's no hope that something can be better, I won't even strive for it. I think that's normal. But I believe that wherever you find yourself right now, whatever problems you may be facing, you can be better, do better, and live a better life.

I'm not talking about just feeling better. There's a difference between feeling better and being better. You need to look no farther than Hollywood to see the difference. The stars of the screen and concert scene seem to have everything they would need or want—power, popularity, money—and yet so many of them seem miserable. They can't stay married or remain faithful to their spouse; they steal; they betray; they're often addicted to drugs and alcohol. But why? If they have it all, why would they still want to engage in such destructive behaviors? The truth is that those behaviors might feel good for a while, but they don't satisfy the soul.

And so, when we seek help for whatever we face, we tend to look in all the wrong places because we're just trying to feel better, not deal with the root of our problems. So we spend $253 billion every year in the United States dealing with the fallout from alcohol abuse and another $193 billion on the carnage left by other illicit drugs.[4] Or we look to sexual distractions and the pornography industry rakes in $57 billion annually with 43 percent of all Internet users viewing pornographic materials.[5] Not all of us embrace such obviously destructive stuff. A lot of us just tune in on our DVR every night to tune out reality around us. Or we grab a quart of caramel chocolate surprise ice cream to make us feel better. If we feel as if we must face our problems alone, that it all depends on us, it's no wonder hope is hard to find. When our distractions wear off, the emptiness returns and the ache in our soul continues.

We each have our own favorite ways of coping, and that approach might actually make us feel better for a little while. The only problem is that when it wears off, we're left with the same problems we had before. We just feel worse. Perhaps the greatest problem is that a lot of us have ruled out the one option that promises true fulfillment and real solutions.

In 2010, 72 percent of the people surveyed said that religion is losing influence in their lives.[6] The number of people who say that religion is very important is decreasing with each new generation, down from 69 percent with those over the age of sixty-five to only 45 percent for those ages eighteen to twenty-nine.[7]

To be candid, I'm not a big fan of religion either. Given the many stupid things done in the name of religion, I can see why some people want nothing to do with it. (I know that sounds crazy coming from a pastor, right? I'm just saying.) But a relationship with a loving God who has revealed Himself to us in the Bible isn't the same thing as religion.

I believe God wants you to be the best version of you that you can be. That's right. Regardless of how you might feel about Him, God wants the best for you. Jesus plainly says so in the Bible: "I have come that they may have life, and have it to the full" (John 10:10). And He told the woman at the well, "Everyone who drinks this water will be thirsty again, but whoever drinks the water I give them will never thirst. Indeed, the water I give them will become in them a spring of water welling up to eternal life" (John 4:13-14). The image He uses is one of a blessed life that overflows like a fountain onto everything around it. When we choose to feel better in the moment, we settle for a temporary, self-centered high at best. What we really want is God's abundant blessing; what we settle for is just a cheap thrill.

Don't Be That Guy

Samson knew a thing or two about chasing cheap thrills instead of trusting God to deal with the problems he faced. The biblical story in the book of Judges (chapters 14–16) tells us he was set apart by God at birth as someone special, someone gifted with both physical strength and God's unique favor. The kind of person everyone only wished they could be. But at every turn, Samson chose to go his own way rather than trust in God's wisdom to deal with his problems.

When he encountered a dead lion with honey inside of it, he chose to disobey God's instructions not to touch anything dead and hid his mistake from his parents. When his father warned him not to marry an attractive lady who didn't share their faith in God, Samson thought only of what pleased himself. "Get her for me," he told his father. When he lost a bet at his marriage party, he used his God-given strength to murder thirty men in cold blood—just to take their clothes.

His life only went downhill from there. After he ran away for months to pout about his lost bet, he returned to find his former fiancée married to someone else. So, once again, he tried to deal with his problem—a problem he helped create—by doing what felt right to him at the time. In what has to be one of the most creative attempts at revenge, he captured three hundred foxes, tied their tails together in pairs along with a lit torch, and turned them loose among the fields of his enemies. Not surprisingly, the people who lost their crops were not happy. Because they couldn't find him in order to retaliate, they killed his former fiancée and her father using fire, just as Samson had used on their fields.

You probably know how this story ends, don't you? Samson continues to live a self-centered life that ends in the arms of yet another woman, Delilah. After he reveals the source of his strength to her, the Philistines take him captive and take his eyesight. Blind, imprisoned, and alone, Samson caps off his disappointing life in spectacular fashion, using the last of his recovering strength to crush thousands of people in a final desperate act of suicide. Even then, in those final moments as he pushed against those support pillars, the Bible tells us that he thought only of vengeance on those who took his eyes.

You may have known a Samson or two in your lifetime. You may even be reading this and thinking that his story sounds a lot like your own, except for the whole foxes-with-fiery-torches thing. (I'm pretty sure we would have seen that on YouTube by now.) It's a tragic story. And it leaves me with this thought: anyone of us could become a Samson—a self-centered person who tries to deal with whatever we face with our own wisdom and in our own way. We see how that worked out for him. The good news is you don't have to be that guy. You can live a better life by choosing to respond to life's challenges in a better way.

Just a Thought:
Why Doing More Isn't the Answer

Sometimes we think that if we can just do more or be busier, we can solve all our problems. If we can just try harder, we can achieve a better life. Don't get me wrong, there's a place for hard work. More of a place than most people care to admit. But Samson's example shows us that more activity doesn't always produce better results.

Think about it: it must have taken days, if not weeks, to catch three hundred wild foxes. He had to keep the ones he had caught penned and fed somewhere. I still don't know how he managed to tie the tails of the foxes together without being bitten, but it could *not* have been easy. In other words, Samson put a lot of work into plans that only made his problems worse. Sometimes, so do we. Just a thought...

You Can Live a Better Life

I believe most people want to live a better life. We want to do better and be better. Our bodies want to be well, as do our minds and our emotions. Maybe I'm wrong about that or maybe you're an exception. Perhaps your goal every day is to make your life worse. But I doubt it. The question is this: are you willing to do what needs to be done to look beyond the cheap thrills and excuses to the key to a better life—a restored relationship with One who wants the best for you and has the power to take you there?

If so, welcome. You've taken the first step toward living a life of deep fulfillment, true happiness, and authentic joy. But that doesn't mean it will be easy. I'm not offering a pathway to a land of make-believe where angelic beings drop delights every day from heaven. Nor am I promising lots of money and possessions, long life or unprecedented success. That may be God's best for you. It may not.

What I am talking about is a pathway that positions you for God's best in the real world where we live and work and play every day. Because that's where God operates. So I'm not saying that you can snap your fingers and end all the pain tomorrow, especially for those of you who've experienced great loss. And I'm not guaranteeing that all your dreams will come true by next Tuesday, or even next year. We've got way too many teachers and pastors promising instant success, as if God were a get-rich-quick genie just waiting for you to rub the lamp in the right way.

I'm talking about the deeper, more fulfilling success that comes from leaving behind the thinking and behaviors that hold you back and engaging a proven pathway to live a better life. Curiously enough, when we do that, those dreams become far more likely to become reality and that pain easier to transition into joy, not because we pushed some magic button but because we've realigned our lives with God's best for us.

So no matter how big your problems seem to you right now—remember those Apollo 13 astronauts stranded in space—God is bigger than your problems.

WHAT YOU CAN DO NOW

- Do you have any problems? Silly question, right? We've all got them. But what are yours? Although it can feel overwhelming to think of everything that isn't working well in life, you can't address problems unless you're first clear on what they are. Take a moment now to list the big problems you face. Don't worry about finding solutions to them on your own at this point. (Remember how well that worked for Samson?) Just write down the ones that seem too big for you to deal with right now.

- Sometimes we need permission to dream of a life that is better than the one we have now. We've all been hurt or disappointed. To avoid being hurt again, we tend to avoid thinking of how we wish things might turn out. We dismiss such thoughts as day-dreaming or fairy tales and listen to the well-meaning voices telling us to be "realistic." But if we can't imagine a better life, why would we ever want to pursue it?

- God wants you to be the best version of you that you can be. Be honest about what you are thinking and feeling about that statement. Do you believe it? What barriers hold you back from believing that God wants what is best for you?

- How would you describe your relationship with the God who has revealed Himself in the Bible? Don't be concerned if you don't even think you have a relationship. Just be honest about where you stand with God right now as we start this journey together.

2

YOUR PROBLEM
ISN'T THE PROBLEM

"I was born a slave on a plantation in Franklin County, Virginia. I am not quite sure of the exact place or exact date of my birth, but at any rate I suspect I must have been born somewhere and at some time." So begins the story of a great man, Booker T. Washington, as he tells it in his autobiography *Up from Slavery*. "Of my ancestry I know almost nothing...Of my father I know even less...I do not even know his name."

Born into slavery, Washington had problems right from the start—and plenty of them. Although he was freed from slavery at the age of nine at the end of the Civil War, his problems didn't magically go away. Few opportunities were available during the contentious years of Reconstruction in the South. He initially carved out a living by working in the salt furnaces and coal mines in West Virginia. But Washington didn't let his problems discourage him from pursuing an education to better himself. While away at school as a young man, however, his mother died, leaving him very much alone.

At the age of twenty-five, Washington was asked to lead a new school known as Tuskegee Institute. Little more than a few ramshackle hen houses in a poverty-stricken part of Alabama, Tuskegee

Institute had an endowment of only $2,000. But Washington and his students were not discouraged; they began to build a bigger campus with their own hands. Over the more than three decades in which he led Tuskegee, Washington lost two wives to untimely deaths. His first wife's death left him the father of one small child while the second death left him a single father of three.

Washington had ample reason to give up. Instead, his autobiography is a candid but hopeful retelling of how this grateful man rose in prominence to become someone many considered to be the chief spokesperson for the freed slaves in America. He was awarded an honorary master's degree from Harvard in 1896 and an honorary doctorate from Dartmouth in 1901. He became an adviser to and friend of multiple US presidents and a highly successful fundraiser for educational causes. At the time of his death in 1915, the "Wizard of Tuskegee" had grown the school's endowment to more than $1.5 million.

In spite of the problems he faced, Booker T. Washington constantly advanced three virtues: forgiveness, humility, and gratitude. He lived out those values in a way that won him the respect and admiration of people of every race and ethnic background. He realized that his problems were not *the* problem. While he couldn't control all that happened to him, one thing he could control was his attitude. It was the perspective he chose to take about his problems that empowered him to become a great man and a great American. The boy who didn't even know where he was born died as one of the most admired and well-known Americans of his day.

What We're Up Against Today

Booker T. Washington's perspective on the problems that came his way seems to be a rare one these days. Even within the church, a place that should be full of nothing but hope, we tend to complain about our problems: "It's not my fault! Life's not fair!" But this thinking only self-sabotages our best hope for living a better life.

As I said earlier, this proven pathway to a better life may be simple, but that doesn't mean it will be easy. You can do it when empowered by God—and I'll show you how—but you can expect to meet resistance. Some of the greatest resistance to living the life you long for won't even come from without but from within. You could very well be your own worst enemy in this process. That's both bad news and good news: bad because you are the one person you can't escape from and good because you are the one person you can actually change.

The greatest challenge any of us may face is confronting the shortage of hope we find in our culture. It's a phenomenon that is at the heart of the resistance we meet. I don't know if there is a technical term for it, but I call it *learned helplessness*. Learned helplessness means, quite simply, that we have learned to be helpless, that we have learned to have no hope when problems come our way. It's a way of thinking that is more common than we'd like to admit and is more often caught than taught.

When we were kids, we had nothing but hope. When I was a child, I could dream the biggest dreams, and I wanted nothing but to be a professional baseball player. But as we grow, well-meaning people crush those ambitions. They say things like: *Be realistic. You can't do this. We're not those kind of people.* If you grew up listening to your parents or family say, "It's not fair. It's not fair. It's not fair. It's not fair," that's the cry of learned helplessness. It's often followed by the conclusion: "And it's not my fault."

So, when a child listens to Mom and Dad say, "It's not fair," then guess what? They learn that everything they don't like in life is because life is not fair. It has nothing to do with them or anything they can control. Life becomes a series of perceived injustices. *It's not fair that my boss doesn't promote me. It's not fair that they make me work weekends. It's not fair that my teacher gave me a lower grade than I wanted. It's not fair because, after all, it's not my fault. They just don't like me. They're just picking on me.* Imagine where millions of oppressed people might be today if Booker T. Washington had thought that way.

I'm not saying that other people are never truly unfair. Washington experienced more than his share of cruelties. But as long as *they* are the problem, *we* have no responsibility for how we respond to anything. So we learn to feel powerless. This sense of learned helplessness sticks with us. We seem to be pulled toward it like moths to a flame. When pressure comes, we revert to it because it feels comfortable and reassuring.

Even though deep down we feel something isn't quite right with what we're telling ourselves, it feels good in the moment to be free of responsibility. We give up, check out, and just coast into a life we really don't want to live anyway. We surrender to our problems because we've convinced ourselves there are no other options. We find ourselves saying, "I just don't care." No wonder so many of us are depressed. Learned helplessness leaves us with no hope.

What Learned Helplessness Gives Us

This attitude of learned helplessness often produces three tragic results. Although they are not the only consequences of this hopeless mindset, I'm sure you're familiar with them:

Learned Helplessness Results in a Sense of Apathy

After all, if we have no hope of a brighter tomorrow, why would we do anything to change the present? This spirit of indifference is a far cry from the pioneering spirit that shaped this country not so very long ago. But it is all too common today. I see it a lot here in New Mexico, but I'm sure you can find it near you too.

We seem to live in the land of mañana. Tomorrow we will take responsibility for living a better life—tomorrow. But tomorrow never comes. We end up procrastinating our own success because we don't believe we can do anything about it. Instead we choose an apathetic approach that leaves the appearance of hope for mañana but no plan for success today. Perhaps you can relate to this thought from an unknown source: "Tomorrow: A mystical land where 99 percent of all human productivity, motivation, and achievement is stored."

I see this apathy often in the church where many people take advantage of everything everyone else does but refuse to contribute themselves. Don't get me wrong—our Dream Team here at Legacy Church is second to none in tireless, faithful service to others. I couldn't be prouder of each one of them. But we still hear the same complaints here that every pastor and church leader hears. But the people grumbling the most always seem to want to do the least. Instead of pitching in to find solutions to problems, they say, "Never mind. I won't say anything more about it. I don't want to get involved."

The sad situation reminds me of the story Jesus told of the Good Samaritan (Luke 10:25-37). After robbers had beaten a man and left him for dead on the road, two travelers (both religious guys, by the way) passed by. But neither one of them wanted to be bothered to help him. Instead, they crossed to the other side of the road and kept going. No doubt they rationalized their callous behavior the same way many of us would: *What good can I do? I'm not a doctor. That's someone else's responsibility.* But the man who showed care to his neighbor was the one who pitched in with what he had to meet the problem the beaten stranger faced. Rather than helplessly shrugging his shoulders, he boldly stepped into the chaos of someone else's problems.

The apathy that results from learned helplessness produces a defeatist attitude that leaves us feeling that we can't make a difference. But think about this: how do we know we can't make a difference until we try to make a difference? And how are we to know the impact that the difference might make? What if you made a difference in one person's life? Is that not enough? I think so, but I see so many people give up before they even start. They stop believing, stop thinking, and stop doing anything because they're consumed by their problems.

Radio legend Paul Harvey once told a story that stuck with me. It's a tale of one man who chose not to just stand by and watch.

Ray Blankenship was minding his own business one morning when he glanced out the window and saw something that would change at least two lives that day. The drainage ditch outside his house had been flooded with rainwater, and a girl was being swept along in the torrent.

Ray ran outside and along the ditch until he was ahead of the panicked child. He couldn't reach her from the bank, so he jumped into the rushing water and grabbed her arm. As the water continued to churn around them, Ray pulled the girl to safety before the rescuers arrived.

Ray later received the Coast Guard's Silver Lifesaving Medal for his actions. He was especially deserving of the award since he was at greater risk than it first appeared. See, Ray Blankenship can't swim.

"And now you know the rest of the story" as Harvey always said. Can you believe it? Ray jumped into the flooded ditch that day knowing he couldn't swim, but believing that he had to try to make a difference in that little girl's life. With the problems you're facing right now, you might think there's no way anyone would ever award you a medal for much of anything. But then, at one point, neither did Ray.

How to know if you've quit trying. How can you tell if you've embraced an attitude of learned helplessness? Try answering these ten questions to discover where you stand:

1. Have you stopped giving other people the benefit of the doubt?

2. How often do you find yourself thinking there is really little to nothing you can do to improve your life?

3. How often do you find yourself saying "I can't..." or "If only I could..."?

4. Have you become overly skeptical (even downright cynical) about other people's intentions?

5. Do you assume the worst about other people and your circumstances?

6. Do you find it hard to agree with others even when you know they're right?

7. How often do you use passive-aggressive behavior such as procrastination, stubbornness, or sarcastic words instead of confronting challenges head on?

8. Do you label people in authority who hold you accountable as being unreasonable?

9. How often do you use the language of a victim by saying, "If only they had or had not..." or "I can't succeed because someone else..."?

10. How quick are you to point out the flaws in those around you?[8]

Learned Helplessness Results in a Sense of Entitlement

After all, if we are incapable of helping ourselves, someone else must be responsible for helping us instead. And that gives us the right to complain if we don't get the help we think we deserve. We start thinking that we are owed a better life *on our terms*, even though we think we can do nothing to achieve it. All we can do is whine and complain when we don't get what we want.

An entitlement means something is due us, that someone has an obligation to give us something. In our culture today, we have taken tolerance for every form of lifestyle and desire to such an extreme that everyone feels entitled to get something based on who they choose to be or what they choose to do. So we look to the government to give us what we think we deserve and end up with a record number of people dependent on the government for payments of some sort. We look to our employer to provide us with benefits or to guarantee hours and our quality of life. In a January 2014 survey from the Pew Forum, 43 percent of Americans surveyed said that government should do a lot to reduce the gap between the rich and everyone else.[9] In other words, almost half of all Americans think, *I deserve to have what they have. And the government should get it for me.*

We even look to the church to give us what we think we deserve. We had an incident here at our church where one of our pastors attempted to give a benevolence packet to a lady who came to us asking for money for food. She did not attend church anywhere and did not want to go through our simple, longstanding procedures to ensure each person receives the help he or she truly needs. Instead, the lady threw the package down and stomped out in a huff saying, "And you call yourself a church!"

I think we've got it all backward. Almost without exception, no one owes me anything in life. I am the one in debt to others. If I am entitled to anything, it's probably only bad stuff, not good. I owe God for not giving me what I do deserve but for loving me instead, unconditionally and freely. In fact, the Bible says that I owe a debt of love and forgiveness to the people I meet each and every day because of the love and forgiveness God has shown to me (Matthew 18:21-35; Romans 13:8-10). But the worst part about this entitlement thinking is that when we don't get what we think we deserve, we start looking for someone else to blame.

Learned Helplessness Results in a Victim Mentality

After all, if I can't help myself and I think you should help me, then it must be your fault when my life doesn't turn out the way I want it to. It's a perspective that actually makes sense *if* we believe we have no hope. If I embrace this attitude of learned helplessness, my attitude gradually shifts from *What's the point?* to *Somebody should do something for me* to *Not only is it not my fault, it's your fault—I'm just a victim.*

We've gotten far too casual in applying this victim label. To borrow an expression from Bible teacher Steve Brown, this victim mentality is from the pit of hell and it smells like smoke! Yet we see it everywhere today as we assign everyone victim status, deserving of an entitlement of some sort. But as Charles Sykes, author of *Nation of Victims,* notes, "If everyone is a victim then no one is a victim." By assigning victim status to anyone who wants it, we devalue those who are real victims, those who truly face the challenge of responding to some incredibly painful stuff.

It's not my intention to dismiss situations that have true victims, especially where people have suffered harm at the hands of others. Not at all. You may be trying to deal with that pain now. But even true victims have a choice. Even when dealing with tragic circumstances, each of us can choose how to respond to harm done to us, just as Booker T. Washington did. Each of us can choose either to pursue a path to a better life or to embrace the label of victim as our new identity and settle into a life of learned helplessness.

I talk to so many people who think they are victims simply because they didn't get what they wanted. The latest smartphone, the latest clothing styles, the highest-rated college education, a larger house, a vacation, a second car even—so many of us whine about prosperity pain. We live in the wealthiest country in the history of the world and yet, when we don't get more, we think we're the victim. If we're not part of the wealthiest 1 percent, we protest and demand more. This is so pervasive that it seems our whole nation is embracing it. We're self-sabotaging the future of the United States of America with these thoughts: *I can't do anything to improve my life, but I'm entitled to something better because I am a victim.*

It shows itself in envious thinking that takes money from someone working hard in order to redistribute it to those labeled as victims of life circumstances. In that Pew Forum survey I mentioned earlier, 50 percent of people surveyed said that "circumstances beyond an individual's control rather than hard work were the primary cause of wealth or poverty." Now, we all know that sometimes things happen that we can't avoid or opportunities seem to fall into our laps, but 50 percent think one's poverty or wealth is *primarily* someone else's fault? That's crazy.

We hear this victim mindset in jealous cries such as this: *How dare you have a great idea that makes millions of dollars! Don't you know I'm struggling?* To that I say, if you don't want to struggle, stop complaining about your problems—real or imagined. Get up and start engaging the pathway to a better life instead of choosing the path of least resistance, a path of apathy, entitlement, and victimhood.

Ultimately, the person most people blame for the problems they face is God. They think that if God really loved them, He would have given them the life they want in the way they want it, the life they think they deserve. When they don't get it, they conclude that even God must be out to get them. I know because I used to think the same thing.

But if we see God as the cause of our problems, we'll never see Him as the source of the solutions. Then we truly have no hope. If we blame Him, we have no other place to go. We're stuck with our own skewed view of reality, the one that got us embracing this learned helplessness in the first place.

When our perspectives are warped by learned helplessness, we fail to see that God may be giving us exactly what we need, even what we want, if only we had the eyes to see it. That's why this victim mindset destroys us. We want something, such as more income to provide for our family. We even ask God for it. But when God blesses us with an opportunity to take on part-time work to earn more money, we say, "I'm already working forty hours a week, so why would God want me to do that? I'm entitled to my leisure time." Well, because we asked for it, that's why! But we think forty hours is too much because we're entitled to our time for leisure and recreation. And if we must work more, then that makes us a victim.

When we get offended all the time, that's a victim mentality. We're so conditioned these days to be overly sensitive, to be offended over everything. But God's perspective is different. Here's what we find in Psalm 119:165 (AMP): "Great peace have they who love Your law; nothing shall offend them or make them stumble." If we love God's wisdom, we're not easily offended or made to stumble.

But what is the rest of the world teaching us? Just the opposite. We're encouraged to be offended all the time, and if we're not offended about something, we're the ones with the problem. When people play the victim card with me, I tell them that we are not to be offended. We are not to be living by the color of our skin or our economic circumstances. We are to live by God's wisdom, what His Word says—don't be offended.

Here's why: if I'm constantly offended, I'm walking in unforgiveness. According to Jesus in Matthew 18, if I'm walking in unforgiveness, I can't be forgiven by God. Now I know it's not politically correct these days to tell people God says to stop thinking of yourself as a victim, but I'm not trying to get elected to anything. I'm just speaking the truth in love. If I love you, I'll tell you that you can never overcome the problems you face by thinking like a victim.

But here's the problem with blaming others: If we never stop blaming, we can never start changing. Blaming other people for our situation does appear to free us from responsibility in the short term, but it also strips us of the power to take a different path. We end up enslaved to whoever gives us what we want when we willingly surrender our power to take responsibility for our lives.

We self-sabotage when we rule out anything we could do to live a better life. If Booker T. Washington had chosen to throw himself a pity party in the face of his problems, he'd have lost before he even started. And so it is with us. When we choose to blame, we make it impossible to grow and change.

Just a Thought:
How Hard Are You Willing to Work?

Here's something to think about. God loves you, and He wants to bless you, but that blessing might mean opening a door to work more. For many of us, our reaction may be that we don't want to work too much. But according to the Bible, we were created to work. Do you work six days a week from sunup to sundown? No? Then you probably don't work too much.

The opportunity to work hard may be one of the greatest blessings God could ever give you. So what do you do with opportunities that come your way to live a better life when they don't fit with what you think you deserve? Just a thought...

WHAT YOU CAN DO NOW

Nearly all of us have been infected in one way or another by this attitude of learned helplessness. Take a moment to evaluate your own thinking using these questions about the three results of learned helplessness that I highlighted in this chapter.

1. Apathy

- Where do you feel apathy or indifference to the problems of others?

- How often do you find yourself making excuses to yourself for why you can't or won't help?

- Do you often find yourself saying that you will do something about your problems *tomorrow*?

2. Entitlement

- What do you think is owed to you?

- Who do you think is responsible to provide what you think you deserve?

- How many of your problems in life are really the result of "prosperity pain" because you haven't gotten the stuff you want?

3. Victim Mentality

- As you think about the problems you're facing in life right now, how often do you say to yourself, *It's not my fault*?

- To what extent do you think you are in control of what happens next in your life?

- Who do you blame for the problems you face?

I said earlier that "the person most people blame for the problems they face is God." Why do you think that is? Do you find that to be true in your own life?

Make a list of the times you have been offended recently by things other people have done or said. If you believe God's wisdom from 1 Peter 4:8, "love covers over a multitude of sins," how many of those offenses would be better off forgiven and forgotten?

3

IF ONLY
I COULD BE YOU

Our problems can mess with our minds if we let them. For example, I used to hate my job before I entered the pastoral ministry. My patient wife will tell you that when I came home at night after working all day, we would never even talk about it. It was that bad of a problem. And it wasn't as if the problem lasted for just a few months or even a few years. For ten years I worked at a job that drove me nuts—delivering packages all over Tulsa, Oklahoma, for United Parcel Service (UPS). Back then, their slogan was "What can Brown do for you?" Let me tell you, there were plenty of nights you would not have wanted to be anywhere near me when I answered that question.

My discontent with my job really had nothing to do with UPS though. It was a good-paying job that provided for my family— that's more than a lot of folks have. No one was forcing me to work there. Sure, the summers are broiling in Oklahoma, so delivering packages in 90-percent humidity and 100-degree temperatures wasn't my favorite thing to do. Then there were winters so cold that I would take off my boots and put my toes on the heater because they were frozen stiff from trudging through wet snow. I still can't help but shiver just thinking about it.

But the problem was not with UPS. They even tried to promote me to management when I was just twenty-two years old. I was shocked because I would run my mouth all the time. I'd just pop off and say whatever I wanted. I told them candidly, "I'm a little shocked you would ask me to move to management." I'll never forget my boss's reply: "Here's the deal, Steve. Whether you go out happy or mad, you always do your job."

The problem was that it wasn't the job I wanted to be doing. I wanted to be in ministry, to be a pastor. I had a Bible college degree that I wasn't using. The painful truth is that I didn't see my job at UPS as a blessing or even as an opportunity. I chose to embrace the attitude of learned helplessness that I described in chapter 2. In fact, I blamed God for my problem. I thought He was doing something *to* me, not doing something *for* me.

Many friends from my Bible college years were serving in ministry, while I was stuck delivering stuff all over Tulsa. Deep in my heart, I would say, *Why, God? Why is everybody else getting to do what I want to do, what I think You have called me to do? Why are they pastoring and I'm not?* It's not that I was jealous of them or bitter toward them. In fact, a lot of my buddies would call and say, "Hey, I've got this going on in the church. What would you do?" I confess there were many times I'd wonder, *Why am I answering all their questions? I'm not the pastor. I'm the one still stuck on a truck!*

I would get off the phone with my friends and think: *If only I could be you.*

My Crazy, Cross-Eyed Life

Today I serve as the senior pastor of Legacy Church, a thriving church (by God's grace) in Albuquerque, New Mexico, with membership over twenty thousand and many more who attend weekly across three campuses. So now I preach six times every week. And I love it.

But at one point, my own father said that I was the last child he ever expected to be speaking in front of people. I'm sure he wasn't the only one. As a child, I would take an *F* in class rather than speak in public. I would turn in my reports, and the teacher would say, "No, you have to read in front of the class."

"I'm not going to do it," I would say. "You'll have to flunk me because I'm not doing it."

You see, I was born cross-eyed and with double vision. So if I had to look at someone without my glasses, there would be two of them. When people would look at me, they didn't know if I was looking at them or not. And without my glasses, I wasn't sure if I was looking at the right image either. It made for some crazy situations that left me frustrated, shy, and angry.

Those of you who dealt with physical barriers as children know what I'm talking about. I spent a lot of my early years throwing punches at everyone who made fun of me. Because I got so used to being rejected, I became terrified of talking in front of people.

And then I encountered God. When I became born again, God gave me a clear direction in life through a restored relationship with Him. And then He called me to be a preacher. Go figure. It had to be of God because it was the last thing I would have wanted to do.

I wasn't picked as "Most Likely to Succeed" at anything in life. An average student in high school, my goal was just to get through. I didn't really care. Just get through school, go to college, get a degree, and then figure out life. To say I had no motivation would be an understatement.

Looking back, I can see that I was pretty lazy at times, content to drift through life and just let stuff happen. I went to Bible college, started working for UPS, got married, and waited for lightning to strike. I didn't recognize it at the time, but I was embracing the attitude I described in the previous chapter, an outlook of learned helplessness.

Even though I had found new life in Christ, I wasn't happy with my life. God hadn't given me what I thought I deserved. Even now when writing this, I sense those resentful feelings wanting to rise up again. What a spoiled, ungrateful, spiritual brat I was! I would get so discouraged, so disappointed; no matter what was happening, I always felt like a failure. People around me would talk about how much God had blessed me, how much I had, but I could not see it. I was making over nineteen dollars an hour. I had a great wife who loved me, three wonderful and healthy children, and rewarding friendships. I was also officiating basketball, football, and fast-pitch softball to make decent money on the side. It was really not a bad life for a twenty-six-year-old.

The reality is that God was blessing me while I was accusing Him of not caring. My problem wasn't the problem. I felt left out, as if God cared about some but not me. After all, if God cared about me, He'd give me what I wanted, right? So why didn't God like me?

My Unlikely Guide to Unexpected Peace

It took timeless wisdom from an unlikely guide to show me the way forward. I had a great friend named Larry King (not to be confused with the television talk-show host). Larry, not surprisingly, had a mother. What was surprising is that his mom became one of the greatest mentors in my crazy, cross-eyed life. I called this sweet lady "Coach" because that is what she did—she coached me through this season of learned helplessness.

She would often stay up on the phone with me until two or three in the morning, listening to me whine and complain about how life just wasn't working out for me, about how my problems were just too big for me. She would have me read her the Bible. As a retired English teacher, she would correct me if I missed a word or didn't say something correctly. Then she would delve into the passage with me. The crazy thing was that she never got angry with me for constantly whining and complaining. She just loved me—and my family—through it.

She would always talk to me about serving God wholeheartedly wherever He had me. That message was always at the heart of Coach's advice to me: no matter what, always serve God. As I grumbled to her about my problems, one of the things she said to me over and over was, "It could be worse." She was always trying to help me see how good I had it. I was always looking down the road, looking past what I did have to what I didn't have. She said wise things like, "You can't compare yourself with anyone else. God has a plan for each of us. Quit thinking about someone else's plan and be thankful for what you have."

Coach helped me to see that the problem wasn't God or UPS or my circumstances. The problem was me and my perspective. It all came down to the way I felt about me. I was insecure, easily intimidated, and ungrateful. I couldn't see how good God was to me because of my bad attitude. My sense of learned helplessness blinded me to what I really had. I didn't value what should have been precious memories because I was so upset about how I thought God had slighted me. I wish I could have those conversations with Coach back again. She passed away in 1998 after seeing me finally become a pastor in Roswell, New Mexico. But she was right. About everything.

My frustrations all had to do with my comparing myself with others. I seemed to always come up short. When you don't see straight, you really don't appreciate what you have. This is the deception, the self-sabotaging that has destroyed so many lives and families. I would tell my wife, "Why don't doors and opportunities open up for me? What did I do so badly that God doesn't like me? I know I'm not the smartest, the best looking, the strongest—but come on! God, why?" The whole time the answer was that I wasn't appreciative of what He had already given me. How blind I was! I had learned to be helpless, to be a victim.

I thought God hated me when I was at UPS. I really did. I thought, *God, I must have done something really bad.* And the whole time I'm crying and moaning, God's training me in so many ways. And I say this humbly, the same people that I used to think had everything I wanted, today they don't have what I have. God knew better than I did. Once I realized that, everything changed. I had to decide to trust Him no matter what. If He was working all things together for my good as He promised (Romans 8:28), that included even the stuff I didn't think was all that great.

As I think back now, it saddens me to think of the wasted time, the years I spent complaining and accusing God. I can see now how God was training me for ministry and taught me so much—even as I did nothing but complain about it. For example, I learned to take responsibility for my own thinking. I learned to check my attitude whenever I begin to feel helpless in the face of life's problems. I learned that no matter how hard it gets to serve as a pastor, how frigid people may seem or how hot the situation feels, I must get up each and every day, say what I need to say, and do the job God has called me to do.

When I decided that God wasn't the problem, I began to grow and renew my thinking. I began to

- appreciate what I have

- not allow myself to feel inferior to anyone
- see myself as God sees me
- stop comparing myself to others
- slow down and enjoy the moment
- be thankful

As the apostle Paul put it, "I have learned to be content with where I'm at and with what I have" (see Philippians 4:11-13). I remember so clearly the freedom I found when I told the Lord, "If You want me to be a UPS man for the rest of my life, I'm willing and will become the best UPS man I can be."

I quit complaining, started thanking, and found great peace.

The Difference Between Agreeing and Believing

Have you ever driven on a lonely road out in the middle of nowhere? Here in New Mexico we have a lot of roads that you can drive on for hours and never even see another car. Nothing but desert, mountains, and a thin sliver of asphalt as far as the eye can see. Oh, and one other thing: speed limit signs. That's right, even out there in the middle of nowhere the signs read "Speed Limit 65." Whenever I'm driving on those roads, I start to wonder, *Am I actually speeding if there is no one around to see me?*

Now I agree that we should have speed-limit laws to keep everyone safe on the roads. But agreeing *with* something is very different from believing *in* something. If you truly believe, there is no such thing as compromising or negotiating, not even with yourself.

For a long time, I lived as if I agreed *with* God not as if I believed *in* God. Even though I said I was trusting God, I really wasn't. I said I believed that God was working all things for my good, but I didn't live like it. I whined and complained about the problems I faced as if God were not in control, even while I agreed that He had it all covered. I agreed with the truth God revealed in the Bible, but I didn't actually believe in the truth He revealed in the Bible. How do I know? Because if I had actually believed the Bible, I would have lived like it.

It's so easy for us to respond to problems in life in this way, by agreeing instead of believing. We say we believe in God, but we don't follow His instructions for dealing with problems. We say we love Jesus, but we don't live as if we're His disciples. Jesus said this about what it means to believe and not just agree:

> Then Jesus said to His disciples, If anyone desires to be My disciple, let him deny himself [disregard, lose sight of, and forget himself and his own interests] and take up his cross and follow Me [cleave steadfastly to Me, conform wholly to My example in living and, if need be, in dying, also].

> For whoever is bent on saving his [temporal] life [his comfort and security here] shall lose it [eternal life]; and whoever loses his life [his comfort and security here] for My sake shall find it [life everlasting] (Matthew 16:24-25 AMP).

We can say we are disciples of Jesus all day long, but until we are willing to deny ourselves, to set aside our own interests when they conflict with God's plans, we're just agreeing, not believing. We're just nodding at the speed limit sign as we fly by at *whatever* speed we choose. In my own journey, I needed to let go of what I wanted to do in life and ask God, *What do You want me to do, right here and now in the midst of all these problems, even those problems I helped create through my own learned helplessness?*

In many ways, even though I was a Christian, I was treating God as someone I agreed with, not as the Lord of my life in whom I believed. You see, I believe we already have what we need to face the biggest of problems by faith in the promises of God, but we don't act on it. We're just *agreeing* with God's promises. We're not *believing* in God's promises. And there's a huge difference between the two.

What God was saying to me through so many voices in my life was this: You say you believe in me? Prove it.

What I Had to Learn

I used to think, if only I could get the breaks someone else gets, if only I could move to a different location, if only I could make more money, if only I had a certain job, if only I could be someone God loves...It never occurred to me that the problem might have been my perspective. I used to pray, *God, just make me a pastor, let me be in the ministry, and I will be different. I will act differently and think differently.* But that's a lie. When I finally got to be a pastor, I realized very quickly that I was the same person with the same issues.

It's like people who don't manage their money well. They think the answer is to make more money. Wrong! It won't matter how much money you make if you bring the same habits with you. If you can't manage $30,000 a year, you won't manage $100,000 a year either. So it was with me. The more responsibility I was given, the more I whined. The more pressure I felt, the more I complained to God, my wife, and anyone else who would listen.

The truth is that you are who you are wherever you go. You can't wait for a better time or circumstances to be better, do better, and live a better life. You have to start now to make better decisions. But learning to be content is hard work.

When I finally got my chance to be a pastor, I left my UPS job and took what I thought was a significant pay cut to serve in a church in Roswell, New Mexico. Yes, *that* Roswell. The one known for alien abduction stories, UFO sightings, and a gathering place for, shall we say, *interesting* people of all sorts. I call it Roswell, America, because although it's not the end of the world, I'm pretty sure you can see it from there. Don't get me wrong, I loved the people we encountered there, but Roswell is pretty far out there in more ways than one. And not long after we moved there, we discovered that even the large pay cut we had planned on was too much for the church of only seventy-three people.

As I struggled once again with the contentment issues I had brought with me, I attended a conference hosted by Willie George, my own pastor and adviser for the last twenty-five years. I came home to Roswell after the Ministry of Excellence conference and told my wife I was never going back to the conference because I found it so discouraging. I explained to her how I thought that I would never have what Pastor George has in ministry influence and effectiveness. My wife said something that I have never forgotten. First, she asked, "How do you know that you won't have that level of influence?" (She stumped me with that one. She's good at that.). Then she said, "Just do something. We may not be able to do everything right now, but we can do something."

And so we did. We started doing what we could with what we had. We went in and did what we could to our building and classrooms. At the time, some people thought we were geniuses. (It's amazing what a little paint can do!). What I realized then was that the main thing limiting me was my own complacent thinking, my sense of helplessness that I had picked up over the years.

Complacency is settling for the status quo. It's a product of the victim mindset that just says, "I give up." If we're complacent, we've surrendered to whatever the status quo may be. In those despondent moments, we tell ourselves, "This is all I'll ever be," as if we could somehow know that with any certainty. But how do we know what we could be? And even if it is all we will ever be, we should be striving to be the best version of us that we can be.

When I said I could never become a more effective pastor, I believed it with all my heart. But by God's grace, I was wrong. Even if you think you will always be a janitor, then tell yourself that you are going to become the greatest janitor in the world. Tell yourself that you are going to become so good that everyone will wish you were cleaning their toilets.

But complacency is more than just settling for a life full of whatever problems we may be facing. When we are complacent, it's as if we are saying, *I've quit hearing. I've quit growing and learning.* My friend, when that happens, then we've really got problems. Because not even God can teach the unteachable. That's why when I go listen to another preacher, I always believe God can give me something more. That's why the motto for Legacy Church is "Something More." God is so much bigger than we could ever imagine, He can always do something more. But even He can't help us if we refuse to believe there could ever be something more.

And how do we know what God has for us? When I was a disgruntled UPS driver or a disillusioned pastor in Roswell, I thought pastoring a phenomenal church like Legacy was out of the question. I wanted what others had, but didn't really believe it could happen to me. And yet, here I am. My life is living proof that if we are faithful with what we have instead of worrying about what we don't have, who are we to say what God can or cannot do?

That's what I had to learn. That maybe, just maybe, I had it all wrong.

Just a Thought:
To Dream or Not to Dream

For many years I was a dreamer. There's a difference between a person who is a dreamer and a person who has a dream. The dreamer talks a lot about how he wishes things could be, but does nothing. That was me. But the person who has a dream usually doesn't say much. He just gets to work. And gets stuff done. Just a thought...

Are You Agreeing or Believing?

Take a brief self-assessment of your own belief level. Answer these ten questions honestly to get a sense of whether you *agree* or *believe*:

1. Do you look at someone else's life and say, "I wish my life was as good as theirs"?

2. Do you ask, "Why do good things never happen to me?"

3. Do you feel that you are stuck in your life with no choices?

4. Do you need someone else to approve of your decisions before you are OK?

5. Do you often feel unsure of yourself?

6. Do you feel like you can never make a good decision?

7. Do you agree with others just to get their approval and acceptance?

8. Do you think that you are always mistreated by other people?

9. Do you feel that life is not fair?

10. Do you think that God is out to get you?

Our Problem Is Nothing New

The challenge we face is not new. According to the Bible, God's user manual for living our lives and for responding to life's problems, we've been falling into this trap of learned helplessness since Eden. Adam stood by while his wife ate the fruit—and then blamed her for his failure. Eve followed Adam's lead and blamed the serpent, who had nobody left to blame. Ultimately, they both blamed God for their own poor decisions. Adam said, "The woman that You gave me," she made me do it. Eve said, "The serpent You created," he made me do it. In other words, "My hard times are not my fault, God. In fact, they're Your fault."

Adam and Eve's son Cain followed their lead down this path of learned helplessness. When he refused to bring the sacrifices God said would be pleasing to Him, God graciously asked him: "Why are you angry? Why is your face downcast? If you do what is right, will you not be accepted?" (Genesis 4:6-7). And what does Cain do in response? He kills his brother Abel who did nothing but do what he was supposed to do. Cain blamed his problems on Abel because he didn't get what he thought he deserved. Only one generation from Eden and he self-sabotages everything, becoming exiled from his family for life.

But I think one of the most tragic stories in the Bible has to be about a guy who was handed the best in life—until he refused to take responsibility for his choices. His name was Saul. He was tall and handsome, and seemed to have everything going for him.

When God chose him to be the first king of Israel, it was as if he had won the lottery.

And yet on his coronation day, we find Saul already beginning to self-sabotage: "But when they looked for him, he was not to be found. So they inquired further of the LORD, 'Has the man come here yet?' And the LORD said, 'Yes, he has hidden himself among the supplies'" (1 Samuel 10:22). The world is at Saul's feet and he's trying to hide, already listening to the attitude of helplessness that screams within him, "Who am I? I'm just a nobody!"

Saul warmed quickly to the new position, perhaps too quickly. Before long he made a decision that would cost him his kingdom. God had given clear instructions that the king was not to offer sacrifices in place of the prophet Samuel. And yet following a victory by the Israelites, Samuel delayed for a week in coming to offer the sacrifice. So Saul chose to take authority that did not belong to him, as if he were entitled to it, and offer the sacrifice himself. Of course, as soon as he did so, Samuel arrived and confronted him over his disobedience:

> "What have you done?" asked Samuel.
>
> Saul replied, "When I saw that *the men were scattering*, and that *you did not come* at the set time, and that *the Philistines were assembling* at Mikmash, I thought, 'Now the Philistines will come down against me at Gilgal, and I have not sought the LORD's favor.' So I felt compelled to offer the burnt offering."
>
> "You have done a foolish thing," Samuel said. "You have not kept the command the LORD your God gave you; if you had, he would have established your kingdom over Israel for all time. But now your kingdom will not endure; the LORD has sought out a man after his own heart and appointed him ruler of his people, because

you have not kept the LORD's command" (1 Samuel 13:11-14, emphasis mine).

Not only does Saul fail to take responsibility for a decision he made, but notice how quick he is to blame others: *It was the men. It was you, Samuel. It was the Philistines that forced me to do it—I'm just a victim of my circumstances. I had to do it. I had no choice.* But God did not agree.

We see Saul slipping further into a state of learned helplessness in the familiar story of David's encounter with Goliath. Because many of us are so familiar with the story of the young shepherd taking on the giant with five smooth stones and a slingshot, it's easy to forget Saul's apathy. He sat by for forty days and did nothing while Goliath taunted Israel.

Some historians and medical experts now tell us that Saul may have had a distinct tactical advantage in this situation. Goliath was a giant, to be sure, but he likely suffered from severe medical challenges that made anything other than close, hand-to-hand combat extremely difficult. The most logical tactical response to engage a foot soldier like Goliath would have been to counter with the weapon that would be the equivalent of the rifle of a modern-day sniper—the slingshot. No doubt, the Israelite army had plenty of slingshot snipers who could have eliminated the threat. But Saul didn't see it. Because David believed success was possible through God, he saw the opportunity that Saul missed as he wallowed in helpless apathy.

When David rightly receives praise for his victory—and many more that follow—Saul becomes envious, thinking he's entitled to praise even if he didn't do the work to achieve the victories. For the next fourteen years, Saul devotes his life to chasing David around the wilderness trying to kill him. Rather than take responsibility for his own destructive decisions, he puts the label "It's David's fault!"

on just about everything. Saul chooses to see himself as a victim of David's success. But all David did was kill the giant terrorizing the very people Saul was supposed to be protecting, a giant Saul assumed he was helpless to defeat.

Before we get too tough on Saul, isn't that what we often do? What I did for many years? We stand by, refusing to deal with our challenges, and then get envious of others who do tackle those challenges and succeed. We even blame them for our own mistakes or lack of success and demand that they share it with us, that we're somehow entitled to some of it simply for existing. In many cases, we flash the badge of victimhood as if that justifies our behavior. Even when others go out of their way to help us, as David did for Saul, our learned helplessness consumes us and keeps us from ever experiencing a better life.

If There's Hope for Me, There's Hope for You

I don't want you, or anyone for that matter, to be like Saul. And I would never want anyone to be like me back then as a frustrated UPS driver. I want something so much better for you. God wants something better for you.

Right now you may be feeling hopeless, overwhelmed by whatever you are facing. But recognizing our limitations does not mean we have no hope; quite the opposite. It's only when we realize our limits that we can begin to discover hope, because that is where God is waiting for us, at the end of our own strength, to empower us to grow and change. In fact, the Bible says this: "Without faith it is impossible to please God" (Hebrews 11:6). He longs for us to not just agree but to believe in Him, to trust in His wisdom to fix our messed-up lives.

When we see life from God's perspective, we see that the challenges we each face are really just opportunities for God to do what

He does best—empower us for another chance. After all, He is the God of *another chance*—not the god of a second, third, or even tenth chance, but *always* another chance. Always. It's when we think we're out of options that God whispers, "Trust Me. Lean on Me. Find hope and strength through Me. And follow My lead."

If like Saul you're headed down the path of learned helplessness, you will not find the success and the joyful life you want. I've been there, done that. If you refuse to take responsibility for the decisions you've made, you can't get there from here. Yes, maybe you've had a rough life—you were abandoned, abused, rejected, and belittled. I'm not saying these things aren't hard to overcome. What I am saying is that we don't get do-overs; we don't get to go back in time and relive them. As Stephen Covey famously described it, those things are within our circle of concern but outside our circle of control.

You can respond to your problems either with envious, self-sabotaging behavior that enslaves you or you can find freedom from the past by taking control of your future. By following God's wisdom, you don't have to keep reliving your pain. You can choose an expiration date for the hold that hurt has over you. You can choose a different path, a hopeful path, God's path for your life.

So you can stay here and wallow in self-pity, or you continue on this journey and let me introduce you to hope.

It's your call.

WHAT YOU CAN DO NOW

- *Be willing to judge yourself.* And be realistic in your judgment. Think of the age-old picture of Lady Justice, blindfolded and holding a balance in her hand. The scale doesn't lie—unless it's been tampered with. It weighs and displays its findings openly. A mindset guided by the Holy Spirit doesn't lie either—unless it's been tampered with. Don't allow self-pity, complacency, or apathy to tamper with your ability to judge yourself in light of God's Word. Prayerfully ask God to work in your thoughts so you can get a true picture of who you are, how you think, and how you need to change.

- *Be honest with yourself.* You may be able to trick everyone else, but there's really no point in deceiving yourself. The Bible says that "if you listen to the word and don't obey, it is like glancing at your face in a mirror. You see yourself, walk away, and forget what you look like" (James 1:23-24 NLT). I've known some guys who look in the mirror and see Brad Pitt when they really look more like George Costanza from *Seinfeld.* Tell yourself the truth and save yourself a lot of trouble.

- *Be willing to be wrong.* If you're on the wrong path, the only way to find the right path is to abandon the one you're on. Start looking for a better road. It's not the end of the world! In fact, it's likely the beginning of your better life. It's OK to admit you have been wrong. It is better to *do* what's right than to always *be* right. Be willing to be wrong, and you'll be *right* in your attitude, *right* in your humility, *right* in your walk with the Lord.

4

HOPE HAS A NAME

I t was the darkest hour for all of humanity, not just for Adam and Eve. After starting their existence walking with God each and every day in the Garden of Eden, our first parents did something that I can only describe as stupid. They did the one thing God had told them not to do. They listened to the false promises offered by a talking snake (empowered by Satan), ignored the promises given by their Creator, and plunged us all into misery. It wasn't as if they could claim ignorance; God had made clear what the price would be for disobedience—certain death and separation from Him forever. In the time it took to decide to take the fruit and eat it, all hope was lost for all of us.

The Bible tells the familiar story of what happened next in Genesis 3. God came looking for his new best friends and found them hiding, ashamed to be seen by Him in their sinful state. And then the blaming began for the problems they faced. Adam blamed Eve. Eve blamed the serpent. Everybody blamed God when all He had done was to create a paradise and put them in it!

But then God said a few unexpected things, because God is at His best when our problems can't get any worse. First, He confirmed the bad news. Death was coming. He had told them that if they ate the fruit, they would surely die. Disobeying God brings unavoidable consequences.

But now God told them that while we would all indeed die, it would not be right away. He would let us continue to live and work on His earth, but it was going to get harder—a lot harder. Now instead of the earth making life easy for us, we'd get quite the workout just trying to survive. But at least we'd get to live. That was good news.

For the woman specifically, God graciously let life continue. She would still be able to bring the miracle of new life into the world, but it was about to get (you guessed it) a lot harder.

As for the serpent who tempted them to disobey—well, that's where something completely unexpected happened. You see, Satan had already rebelled against the Creator prior to Adam and Eve entering the scene. In his ongoing struggle against God, Satan had seized this opportunity by taking on the form of a serpent in some way. So when God addresses the serpent here, He isn't just talking to a snake but to the Great Deceiver himself. God said,

> "I will put enmity
>   between you and the woman,
>   and between your offspring and hers;
> he will crush your head,
>   and you will strike his heel."
>   (Genesis 3:15)

For those trying to make sense of the poetic language used by the writer of Genesis, let me translate. God declared that the conflict between Himself and Satan would now include us. There would now be conflict between those who trusted God and those who followed Satan by going their own way. This struggle would serve as the backdrop of history. So it was when it seemed things couldn't possibly get any worse for us, hope arrived in these words to Satan: Hope will crush you.

The Hebrew word translated "offspring" in the passage above is a proper noun, indicating God wasn't just talking about general opposition to Satan but a very specific resistance. Someone was coming. A very particular Someone. He would be born of a woman and would finally destroy the power of the serpent forever. Satan would "wound his heel," but this promised Someone would deliver a mortal blow to the Great Deceiver that would end the conflict once and for all.

Talk about good news! Into the midst of our greatest failure come good tidings of great joy. That's why Christmas is such a big deal. That's why hosts of angels made such a fuss about the birth of a little Someone who could finally bring peace to us all. That's why we sing carols like this one every December:

> Hark! the herald angels sing,
> "Glory to the newborn King!"
> Peace on earth, and mercy mild,
> God and sinners reconciled.
> Joyful, all ye nations, rise,
> Join the triumph of the skies;
> With the angelic host proclaim,
> "Christ is born in Bethlehem."
>
> Christ, by highest heaven adored:
> Christ, the everlasting Lord;
> Late in time behold him come,
> Offspring of a virgin's womb.
> Veiled in flesh, the Godhead see;
> Hail, the incarnate Deity:

Pleased, as man, with men to dwell,
Jesus, our Emmanuel!
Hark! the herald angels sing,
"Glory to the newborn King!"

Hope has a name—Jesus. Hope was born in a manger in Bethlehem. Hope lived and walked among us. Hope isn't something you'll find in the self-help section of your local bookstore. It isn't something you get from a therapist, a politician, or even a pastor. Hope is a person—a person who lived, died, and came to life again. Jesus didn't just give hope. He is hope, the Someone promised in Eden so long ago. He came to restore what was broken, to mend the relationship with God that was shattered by our first parents' mistakes. And so He did what only hope could do. He gave Himself for you.

Just a Thought:
God's Way or the Hard Way

Maybe it's just me, but there seems to be a pattern in life. We see it not just in Eden but throughout all of life. Do things our own way instead of God's way and we get a life that is a lot harder. Jesus said that the way is broad that leads to our own destruction and there are many people on it (Matthew 7:13-14). Is it any coincidence then that we have so many problems today as individuals, as families, as a nation? When we insist on doing things our way instead of God's way, we get problems. As Dr. Phil would say, "How's that working out for you?" Maybe we should rethink that strategy. Just a thought...

Where Hope Lives

"Hope is the thing with feathers that perches in the soul." Have you heard that expression before? With all due respect to Emily Dickinson, the poet who wrote those words, I just don't think feathers in the soul are what we need when facing big problems. I think most of us are looking for real hope in the real world. And in the real world, feathers just don't cut it. We need something more. We need hope that is bigger than our problems, the kind of hope that my friend Melvin found to face some really tough stuff.

When I think of all the people I've known who've found hope in the midst of overwhelming challenges, few have had to face more problems than Melvin. Last year Melvin called our Dream Team coordinators at Legacy Church with an apology. He wouldn't be able to make it to the Wednesday evening service where he was scheduled to serve as an usher. Now we've heard a lot of excuses for not showing up to serve. And we get it. Life happens. Stuff comes up. But Melvin's apology was a first: "I won't be able to make it to serve as an usher at church tonight. My leg is being amputated."

Perhaps I should back up and share a little more of Melvin's story to put that call into context. Melvin was born in East Los Angeles and spent the first twenty-eight years of his life in and around Long Beach. Although he was raised Catholic, he didn't go to church much. He said he believed in God, but it didn't really affect how he lived his life. His mother tried her best to steer him in the right direction, but by his own admission, Melvin thought he knew better and made his own choices—choices that landed him in prison in 2008 for selling drugs.

A capable attorney got his nine-year sentence reduced to three years with half time, but his poor choices continued. When he fell in with a rough crowd in prison, his situation went from bad to worse. Here's how he describes it:

> Not more than a year after I went in, I got in a big prison riot. There was so much chaos going on—mace, tear gas bombs, all that stuff. Somehow I got hit in the back of the head. Everything went completely white. They put me in a little cage to wash me off, and it was then that I discovered that I couldn't see. At first I thought it was the chemicals they had used on us. When I finally started blinking again, I got back my sight but only in one eye. The other one was done for. I was blind in one eye, and the one that still worked had lost all peripheral vision.

But even as Melvin's choices led to limited physical sight, God began opening his eyes in other ways. He started to attend the prison ministries. Every Sunday when the prison was not in lockdown, Melvin went to church and began to find hope. He got his GED and started serving other people through a prison program that helped inmates prepare to reenter the work force. He began serving as a demonstrator, talking to other inmates about the harmful effects of drugs and alcohol. When he was finally paroled, he knew he had to get away from the relationships and lifestyle he had known before, so he moved to Albuquerque.

Soon he was working some construction jobs with his nephew. But problems followed him here. You see, Melvin has been a type 1 diabetic since the age of eleven. Not that he let that condition influence his lifestyle much. He still ate tons of candy, drank sodas and alcohol freely, and smoked marijuana—all the stuff that a diabetic shouldn't have been doing. As a result, his health wasn't that great and his immune system was pretty depleted. While on a job with his nephew, a nail punctured his foot and penetrated deep inside his ankle. He was rushed to the hospital for a tetanus shot, but a week later his ankle was the size of a grapefruit with an infection called osteomyelitis. First they cut off his big toe on that foot. Soon they had to cut off all the toes to try to keep the infection from spreading.

Melvin was beginning to spiral downward into despondency. He describes what happened next:

> I was fed up with Albuquerque. I was like, *I'm done. I don't need to be here. I can go back to California and do whatever I need to do back there.* I called my dad from the Greyhound bus station to let him know I was coming home. I got on the bus while talking to a buddy on my phone, but something made me say to him, "Well, let me get off and go to church first to see what God tells me."

> I had already been attending Legacy Church for a little while and even pitching in and helping out. But that next Sunday we had a special speaker at church, Bishop Bonner from Atlanta; it was like somebody called him and told him, "Melvin's going down. Make sure you make the service about him." Because that's how it felt.

> I had limped into that service in more ways than one. But this is what I remember him saying: "Even though you are limping or even though you're going through whatever you're going through, whenever you start something, you have to finish it."

> Those were his words to me that day. And that is where I came to meet Jesus. I heard that message, and from that point on I just stuck with it. I decided to stay and see what God was going to do.

Melvin's body lost the battle with the infection. In March 2012, his leg was amputated just below the knee. Six weeks later, he was back in church just in time for Easter.

It was during physical therapy that he met a lady named Rita who worked in medical records. A single mother with two daughters and a history of abusive relationships, she knew a thing or two about problems. For a dozen years prior to meeting Melvin, she was angry with God about her life. In fact, the day before meeting Melvin, she had cried out to God, "That's it! I can't do it anymore. I'm done!"

The very next day she met Melvin. He began talking about his newfound faith in God. He told her of his trust in God to do what is best and of his hope to keep moving forward. She saw it as an answer to her prayer, a sign that God still cared for her. As she got to know Melvin more, she realized there was something different about him. Here's how she described the impact he had on her and her two daughters:

> He started talking to me about going to church. Even while he was in the hospital, he cared about others. He asked if I could go and buy gifts for Toys for Tots. No matter what his situation, no matter what he was going through, he still thought about everybody else. No matter what he did, Melvin honored God. He'd come to church every Wednesday, every Sunday, serving, regardless if he was walking or in a wheelchair, sick or not sick, having a good day or a bad day, he was there.

> He put God first in everything, so it made me want to do that. It made my faith stronger. It made my kids' faith stronger. After twelve years of desperation, within weeks of starting to come to church with Melvin and hearing God's Word from Pastor Steve, our faith grew stronger and everything changed.

The bottom line? Melvin and Rita discovered hope, and countless others have followed their example. Melvin's faithful service in spite of his problems has moved many people at Legacy and in our local community to step up.

In August 2013, Melvin and Rita got married. They began serving together both in and out of church, preparing to launch a new ministry called You Can, Too! that would inspire and help people to overcome physical disabilities.

But Melvin had another challenge yet to come. It was the one that prompted that phone call to the church in early 2014 that I mentioned earlier. On top of everything he had endured, an infection was about to claim his one remaining leg.

This time as they prepared for surgery, the prognosis looked grim. The doctors told Rita that Melvin's kidneys were failing. The infection in his bloodstream was spreading. He might not survive. Rita recalls crying out to God and praying over Melvin with their church family and friends. Two days later the doctors gave a very different report: the infection was gone. They couldn't understand how or why, but it was gone. God had stepped in. A week later, Melvin was headed home.

So here's a guy who went to prison, lost an eye, has limited sight in his remaining eye, has Type 1 diabetes, first lost his toes, then a leg, and finally both legs—and all of it has only strengthened his faith in God. What's up with that? He continues to trust that God has whatever he needs for whatever he may face.

Far from settling for an attitude of learned helplessness, Melvin refuses to quit—not because he is great, but because God is greater than his problems. As his wife puts it, "Not having legs does not stop him. He does anything his heart desires." The hope within him seems only to grow stronger with each new challenge that comes his way.

And Melvin's take on what he has endured? "I'm just thankful God is using me as a vessel to help others. I tell people so many times that I think I sound like a broken record. Losing my legs is so little compared to what I have gained. I've gained God and so many other people in my life that it's just been amazing. I mean, fall after fall, dealing with diabetes, all of it—it's all been making me stronger."

Melvin's perspective sure doesn't sound like someone who's embraced an attitude of learned helplessness. It doesn't sound like apathy. I've never known anyone—with or without legs—to be more dedicated to serving others. It doesn't sound like entitlement to me, either. I've never known anyone to be more humble and grateful in the face of such problems. Melvin sure doesn't sound like he's embraced a victim mentality. He has chosen instead to overcome his problems by faith in the One who loved him and gave Himself for him.

Melvin believes the promise of God that He rewards those who diligently seek him. He believes in God's promise that He will work all things—even prison, diabetes, and amputated legs—for good for those who love Him. Melvin doesn't just agree with those promises; he believes them. And so he proves it each and every day.

When We Let Hope Lead

I said earlier that if we see God as the cause of our problems, we'll never see Him as the source of our salvation. Melvin certainly had plenty of excuses to blame God for the problems that came his way. But if he had blamed God, he would never have found the unbelievable hope that now empowers his life and inspires so many others.

If we blame God, we have no other place to go because He is hope. The Bible even refers to Jesus by that name—the blessed hope (Titus 2:11-14). It says that we have come now to a living hope (1 Peter 1:3-4), not stale truths tucked away in a theological tome somewhere, but a relationship with a dynamic and powerful person.

Unfortunately, so many of us are committed to seeing things the way we want to see them. We're committed to thinking like I thought at one time—if God really loved me, He would do this for me, or if He really cared, He wouldn't let that happen to me.

The key to connecting with God as the source of hope is understanding that we are not in charge in the first place. The apostle Paul puts it bluntly in Romans 9:20 (AMP): "But who are you, a mere man, to criticize and contradict and answer back to God? Will what is formed say to him that formed it, Why have you made me thus?" Yet isn't that exactly what we do? We question God and demand answers and action on our terms. And that's exactly why we never seem to see any progress dealing with our problems. When we let hope lead, our lives become, not surprisingly, more hopeful.

Real change happens when we totally surrender our will to God's will, when we lay down what we want so He can give us what we need. Unfortunately, we live in a world where even in the church we want conditional surrender. We want to be able to negotiate life—and even death—on our terms.

We even want to negotiate our relationship with God. We think, *how little do I have to commit and still get into heaven?* It's as if we think of God as the banker in *Deal or No Deal* whose stingy offers we can refuse in the hope of something better. As if God is keeping us from the joyful life we seek. We wonder, *what level of commitment will God take as the minimum offer?* The answer is that He will accept nothing less than everything. We cannot negotiate our way to Christ or come to Him little by little when it's convenient for us.

There is a dangerous thinking in the Christian church today that gives people a false sense of security. It goes like this: *If I just pray a prayer, ask God to forgive me, and believe that Jesus is real, then somehow that will be enough.* What Jesus Christ taught and what the

Word of God teaches is total, unconditional surrender. We don't get to negotiate the terms with God. It's not as if we can just cancel our subscription when we feel like it. That's not how it works. We're either all out or all in. Jesus describes the final outcome for those who've only partially surrendered:

> "Not everyone who says to me, 'Lord, Lord,' will enter the kingdom of heaven, but only the one who does the will of my Father who is in heaven. Many will say to me on that day, 'Lord, Lord, did we not prophesy in your name and in your name drive out demons and in your name perform many miracles?' Then I will tell them plainly, 'I never knew you. Away from me, you evildoers!'" (Matthew 7:21-23).

When He says "on that day," He is referring to the unavoidable day of judgment we all must face. When these partially surrendered people list the many good things they think they have done for Jesus, His response will be stern: "I never knew you." How could that be? Because they had surrendered conditionally, not totally. They were willing to follow Jesus for this and that, but not for everything. Jesus is saying, "You looked the part, but I never had your heart. You agreed outwardly, but you didn't believe inwardly. Because of that, I have no real relationship with you."

Apart from full surrender, we remain an enemy of God, stuck in the aftermath of Eden's mistakes. In short, we are not truly saved. We may agree that Jesus is in charge, but the Bible says that even Satan and his demons do that. The question is: Have you submitted your will to Him completely?

This phenomenon of conditional surrender is why so many people who call themselves Christians have such a hard time doing the simplest things God requires: be part of a local church, serve in that local church, and give to that local church. Why are these so difficult for so many? The answer is pretty straightforward: They are unwilling to submit their will to Christ.

Hope Starts with Surrender

Have you ever heard someone say, "I have a strong-willed child"? That expression is usually code for having a child who refuses to obey. When my children were younger, I had to discipline them often. I loved them and knew they needed to submit to my direction to live a better life. A strong-willed or disobedient child rejects a parent's instruction. Tell him or her "Don't do this" or "Don't touch that," and the child will look you right in the eyes and do it anyway. They are not submitting their will to the authority in their lives and they often reap painful consequences.

Yet so many professing Christians do the same thing. They refuse to submit to the authority of God's Word. Here's the problem: if we don't surrender to God's direction for our lives, then we have no hope for true salvation. Praying a prayer without any desire to live differently doesn't change anything. Someone may learn to hide sin better, but is there any real conviction to stop doing it?

Conditional surrender to God may seem attractive at first until we realize that there is no such thing. Imagine if Nazi Germany had only partially surrendered at the end of World War Two. How would that have worked if they had agreed to stop invading mainland Europe but still continued to bomb England every so often? It wouldn't have worked at all, of course, because it would not truly be surrender. Surrender is always and only total. I agree with John C. Maxwell who says, "Either God is Lord of all or not Lord at all."

Today so many people are teaching that coming to Christ is a process. It's not. They teach that we can gradually transition into

following Jesus at our own pace. We can't. Overcoming our character issues, rising above a victim mentality, dealing with rejection and
abandonment issues, growing in the grace and knowledge of God—
those things are part of the process that follows as a natural result
of the new relationship with God. But coming to Christ is an all or
nothing proposition that changes you immediately.

The apostle Paul says, "Anyone who belongs to Christ has
become a new person. The old life is gone; a new life has begun!"
(2 Corinthians 5:17 NLT). When you truly give control of your life
to God, your desires change. You become convicted immediately
when tempted to disobey.

Just a few days after I surrendered my life to Christ's direction,
I was driving by myself in my car. I started to light up a cigarette,
but immediately had this thought: *Don't smoke it. It's not good for
you. Throw it out.* I didn't know enough about God to think that
He might be speaking to me. It was just a thought, but it was a different type of thought. It was powerfully convicting. So I put that
cigarette back in the pack and chucked the whole thing right out
the window. (Apparently I wasn't as convicted about littering then
as I would be now.) I never smoked another cigarette again. God
changed my desires; He freed me from that addiction because I had
given Him my heart without reservation.

Other things started to change as well. I was a pretty immoral
guy prior to coming to Christ. So one of the first thoughts I had
at that time was that I needed to stay away from temptation with
girls. I knew I would only get into trouble. One day when I came
out of the bank, a girl I knew very well approached me and asked
where I had been. I told her I had been going to church. I was leaning on a car at the time; she came close to me and started rubbing my
chest. She told me she would like to see me that night. I was totally

freaking out. I didn't really know what to do. I only knew that every alarm in my soul was going off!

But then a thought came to me about Joseph. I hadn't been saved that long, so I knew almost nothing about the Bible. I knew enough to know that what she was suggesting would be wrong. I had heard the preacher at a recent service teach about Joseph running from his master's wife when confronted by a similar situation. So as this very pretty young lady was trying to convince me to come over to her house, I had one thought: *Run.* So I ran, literally. I took off running, jumped in the car, and got out of there. It's all I could think of doing. She probably thought I was the craziest person in the world, but it didn't matter to me. I didn't want to keep sinning. I had totally surrendered my will to God's authority. As I began to get to know God better, He empowered me to deal with a lot of other stuff that was keeping me from being the best version of me that I could possibly become.

Apart from total surrender, we have no hope for truly dealing with our problems. We have no real salvation. That's why so many people never get help with the problems they face. They never get delivered because they never totally surrender to the One who offers hope to all who truly believe.

In today's culture, God is offered as one option among many to help you cope with your problems. There's therapy, medication, vacations, and—oh yes, God. Even many church leaders no longer believe in the power of God to change lives and heal our wounded hearts. As Timothy describes it, they have embraced a form of godliness, but they deny God's power to transform (2 Timothy 3:5). They agree but they don't believe. They've become acclimated to church rather than surrendered to Jesus.

But Jesus reserved some of His harshest words for those who

embrace a message of half-hearted surrender: "those of you who do not give up everything you have cannot be my disciples" (Luke 14:33). Jesus is quite clear about what it will take to follow Him, to have the hope only He can give—all or nothing.

Are You Ready to Live?

So what's it going to be? Are you out or in all the way? The pathway to a better life starts at the foot of the cross where hope gave Himself for you. Apart from knowing Jesus, our living hope, you have no hope in this life or eternity to come. Even if you should accomplish great things by your own strength, you will lose your soul.

Following Christ without reservation doesn't mean we won't make mistakes. It doesn't mean we will be perfect. Not at all. But it does mean that we will recognize and repent when we do fall short. If we give our hearts and minds to God, we will truly experience God's power.

God is a kind God. He wants the best for us. But He is a perfect gentleman and comes only where He is invited. It all begins with giving God permission to breathe hope into your life no matter the problems you face right now. God is bigger than your problems. He is bigger than your mistakes. Regardless of your present circumstances, the Bible says you can begin again right now: "If you declare with your mouth, 'Jesus is Lord,' and believe in your heart that God raised him from the dead, you will be saved" (Romans 10:9).

We will be saved from sin's sorrows and restored to a right relationship with our Creator if we truly believe and confess the truth about Jesus, the promised hope. If you are ready to begin a better life, one surrendered to the one the Bible describes as the giver of all good things, take a moment now to put the following simple statement into your own heartfelt prayer:

*God, I believe that Jesus is the Son of God, the hope that you
promised in Eden. I believe that He came to earth to die in
my place for my sins and to crush sin and Satan. I believe
that You raised Him from the dead on the third day to reign
forever, just as You will cause me to live forever with You for
all eternity. I believe these things in my heart and confess
with my mouth that Jesus is now the Lord of my life.*

If you prayed this prayer, you are on your way to becoming the
best version of you that you could possibly be. You are a new creation, not perfect, but fundamentally transformed from the inside
out. You've had a spiritual DNA change. Like Melvin, you now have
an unshakeable hope that no matter the problems you face or the
mistakes you have made, your God is bigger.

Your hope now has a name—Jesus. And He's not just the Maker
of the universe in which you live; He's your friend too.

WHAT YOU CAN DO NOW

- Did you pray to make Jesus the Lord of your life? If so, congratulations on your new life in Christ! You've found lasting hope. You are a new creation and your journey to a better life has just begun. But whatever you do now, don't stop reading! The rest of this book will give you critical direction and guide you through proven steps to deal with the problems you face by and through God's unlimited strength.

- Would you call yourself a follower of Christ, but you're not sure that you are all in? Perhaps you've realized now that the life you've been living has been one of *conditional* surrender to God, not unconditional submission to His best for you. If you're not sure where you stand with God, I encourage you to get sure. Pause now and pray. You can use the prayer on page 77 to guide you. Confess and believe. And know with certainty that your hope is here to stay.

- Are you undecided? Perhaps you are not yet ready to trust in Christ as the source of your hope. Can I ask you to do two things? First, keep reading. I've got a feeling that the rest of this book will help you make sense of the many questions you may have right now about how such a relationship can empower you to overcome your problems. Second, ask yourself this question: Where is my hope? Then complete the following statement to help you figure it out: When problems are too big for me, I trust in _____. If your trust is not in a God who is bigger than the problems you face, where is it instead?

- If you already have the relationship with God that I described above, perhaps you have been convicted as you've read about total and unconditional surrender to God. Are there areas in your life that you refuse to surrender to God's control? Those areas may well be the source of many of your problems or they may be keeping God's blessings from flowing generously to you. Take a moment to list areas you need to fully surrender to God's control. Then pray right now and do just that.

5

THE GOD OF ANOTHER CHANCE

After reading the previous chapter about encountering a living hope who can empower you to face your problems, you may be thinking, *I just don't believe it, not for me. Not for the problems I face. If you only knew how much I've messed up my life or how big my problems are right now...* And you wouldn't be the first to think that your problems are so bad that not even God can fix them. That's a club every one of us has joined at one time or another.

The problem with thinking like that is that we are not God, so we don't see things as He sees them. We don't think like He thinks. In one of the most jaw-dropping promises ever made, God promised to work all things for good for those who love Him. The apostle Paul states it as a matter of fact, almost as if he's saying "the sky is blue" when he says, "And we know that in all things God works for the good of those who love him, who have been called according to his purpose" (Romans 8:28). His purpose is to renew and restore you to a right relationship with Himself. He made this incredible promise even though He already knew the problems you would face. Your problems haven't caught God by surprise.

Most of us have painted a picture in our minds of how our life will be, of how it should be. We imagine it in vivid colors as if it were here already. We measure our contentment based on how closely reality conforms to that picture. The problem comes when life turns out differently than what we imagined and yet we still cling to that original painting.

But we are not in total control of the canvas, the paint selections, or all the conditions in which that picture gets painted. Sometimes our picture gets knocked off the easel and trampled into the mud by unexpected events. A tragedy may strike an ugly stain across our design. Storms may soak our canvas for a season, leaving our picture faded and blurred at best.

And so we become bitter. We fall prey to the victim mentality. We accuse God of not loving us as we crumble up our picture and pout in the corner instead of trusting that He has a better picture in mind for us.

I've certainly done that before. During my decade at UPS, I thought God had messed up my life picture, until I learned to be content and trust in His wisdom more than my own. I had to be willing to get out the eraser and modify my timetable to match His. After starting to pastor a church in Roswell that had just shrunk from eight hundred members at one time to seventy-three, I had to scrub off the paint I had applied so I could see what God was creating to help hurting people.

Throughout our lives we may have to revisit the canvas often to create a new picture or modify an old one because—news flash!—we are not God. Ever since Eden, we've been trying to become just like Him, to paint our own reality apart from His control. We paint our own pictures and then get angry when the universe doesn't conform to our imagination.

But how can we grow and learn if we play the victim card when life doesn't turn out the way we want it? People who embrace a victim mentality can't repaint anything. They don't erase and redraw the lines; they just let stuff happen to them.

But I can choose to respond to what God permits in my life by saying, "It is what it is. It happened. Now what will I do about it?" When I repaint the picture, it motivates me to get back up with the light God has given me. I say, "I've got to take a different route than what I had planned, because I didn't see that coming. But God knew it was coming, and He loves me. So I'm good." We must be willing to submit our perspective to God's perspective or we'll end up with a pretty messed up picture.

Is There Hope for You?

When we begin to see life from God's perspective, the challenges we face become opportunities for God to do what He does best—empower us for another chance. After all, He is not the God of a second, third, or even twentieth chance, but the God of *another chance*. Always. When we think we're out of options, we lose hope. It's when we have our picture destroyed and our hopes crushed, that God leans in closer and whispers, "Trust Me. Lean on Me. Find hope and strength through Me. And follow My lead."

One thing I have learned is that God delights in turning *hopeless* into *hopeful*. Consider this account by Luke of how Jesus transformed a woman whose life hadn't worked out the way she had planned:

> As Jesus was on his way, the crowds almost crushed him. And a woman was there who had been subject to bleeding for twelve years, but *no one could heal her*. She came up behind him and touched the edge of his cloak, and *immediately her bleeding stopped* (Luke 8:42-44, emphasis mine).

Here was a woman who was out of options, a woman beyond all human hope. We don't know the details of her illness, but it certainly wasn't what she had imagined for her life. She had tried everything on her own. Finally, after twelve years of hopelessness, she encountered hope and healing when she touched the God of another chance.

But what if your life is a mess because of choices you've made and not because of circumstances beyond your control? Does God offer you another chance too? Consider how Jesus responded to a woman He met in Samaria beside a well. As the discussion turned to the living water that Jesus offered to heal her soul, some interesting facts came to light:

> "Everyone who drinks this water will be thirsty again, but whoever drinks the water I give him will never thirst. Indeed, the water I give him will become in him a spring of water welling up to eternal life."

> The woman said to him, "Sir, give me this water so that I won't get thirsty and have to keep coming here to draw water."

> He told her, "Go, call your husband and come back."

> "I have no husband," she replied.

> Jesus said to her, "You are right when you say you have no husband. The fact is, you have had five husbands, and the man you now have is not your husband. What you have just said is quite true" (John 4:13-18).

Talk about an awkward conversation! Here was a woman whose life had been chaotic to say the least, a soap opera if ever there was one. And at that moment she was living with a guy who was not her husband. But Jesus wasn't done. Notice how the woman describes the rest of her conversation with Jesus:

> Then, leaving her water jar, the woman went back to the town and said to the people, "Come, see a man *who told me everything I ever did.* Could this be the Messiah?"…
>
> Many of the Samaritans from that town believed in him because of the woman's testimony, *"He told me everything I ever did."* So when the Samaritans came to him, they urged him to stay with them, and he stayed two days. And because of his words many more became believers (John 4:28-29,39-41, emphasis mine).

If we read between the lines a little, it doesn't take much imagination to realize what an extremely uncomfortable conversation that must have been if they discussed *everything* she ever did. Nevertheless, all of her mistakes didn't stop Jesus from giving her another chance at a new life. In fact, He turned it into an opportunity to give a lot of other people new life as well.

But that's what God does for those who've messed up. Prostitutes, tax collectors, thieves, lepers, murderers—all people with problems. These are the people Jesus ran toward. The religious leaders of the day mocked Jesus and His disciples for being seen with people they had labeled as unclean, unfit, and hopeless. But Jesus responded, "Those who are well have no need of a physician, but those who are sick. I did not come to call the righteous, but sinners, to repentance" (Mark 2:17 NKJV). Jesus came to heal and give hope to the hopeless. He came to deliver us, to take our labels off, and lead us into a joyful life beyond what we can imagine.

We may think that labels from our past mistakes define us: loser, adulterer, addict, abuser, victim, liar, gossiper, failure—the list goes on. The world around us joins in, slapping labels on us to keep us where it thinks we should be: victim, felon, underprivileged, minority, disabled, poor, and so forth. As if that weren't enough, Satan himself specializes in applying labels—with super glue. As the originator of the victim mentality, he thinks if he can control our perspective, he can destroy our hope. And he's right. Labeled and hopeless—that's exactly where the enemy wants us.

But God is always trying to take our labels *off*. He makes incredible promises to show us we do not have to settle for the labels we wear right now:

- "Everything is possible for one who believes" (Mark 9:23).
- "With God all things are possible" (Matthew 19:26).
- "If you have faith as small as a mustard seed, you can say to this mountain, 'Move from here to there,' and it will move" (Matthew 17:20).

God doesn't say these things again and again in His Word because *He* needs to hear them. It's for *our* benefit, because we see ourselves through the distorted lens of learned helplessness. We struggle to believe God could love us enough to give us another chance. We struggle to see ourselves as anything other than victims. We struggle to think that God would care enough about our problems to move heaven and earth to help us.

But no matter what labels you might be wearing today, God sees something different when He looks at you, someone He loves and longs to embrace once again while wearing the only label that matters—His friend.

God Takes Our Labels Off

Labels can be powerful things. I once had a friend who led a private school tell me of an incident that demonstrated the power of labels to define how we see ourselves. One day while he was welcoming the incoming students to the school, he met a new middle school student. As she greeted him in the hallway, she gave her name (I'll call her Susan) and then immediately followed with her label: "I'm Susan. I'm dyslexic." My friend was shocked and gave her a puzzled look before responding, "You can leave your labels at your previous school. Here you are just Susan. Welcome."

Over the next six years, my friend watched the young lady blossom both as a student and as a leader. She started believing that she was more than the label that had been assigned to her. After she graduated as a member of the National Honor Society, he told me that he couldn't resist scribbling a message on her graduation photo: "If only you believe..." That's not to say her academic challenges weren't real. She probably had to work a lot harder than most students. But her problems began to shrink when she became part of a school community that saw her as God saw her—without the labels.

Brother Haymes was another friend who served for many years on our church board of directors here at Legacy Church. Prior to that, he was one of the men who had hired me to pastor in Roswell. He has since passed on to eternity, but he had a son who was labeled at birth as retarded (a more acceptable term in those days). The experts told his parents that their son would never learn, never grow, and never fully develop into a productive member of society. But his family refused to give up hope. They refused to allow labels to define their son. Brother Haymes told me, "Pastor Steve, we just didn't believe it. We refused to believe it. We worked with him and worked with him." Today their son is a college professor. His family chose to see him as God saw him and to empower him to live a label-free life.

One of the labels I've struggled with a lot is being a "nobody." As I grew up and even after I had begun a new relationship with Christ, I didn't think I deserved much of anything. I thought, *Why would God ever help me. Who am I?* My conclusion was always that I wasn't worth it, that I was a nobody. Because I wore that label, I didn't expect much from God or anyone else. As a result, I was easily intimidated. I felt like a failure and wouldn't even try to succeed. When I would get around people who I thought were important, I would get tongue-tied and say the dumbest things. I'd end up feeling stupid and walk away thinking, *I knew it. I am a nobody.*

What I learned over time is this: none of it was true. I projected my own insecurities onto God and made myself a victim of that projection. Even though I was serving God at the time, I was mostly just trying to get Him to like me. When I started to let His Word and not my own insecurities and fears direct my thinking, I stopped being a victim. Everything changed.

When I began looking at the promises of God in His Word, I realized that I had been asking the wrong question. Instead of asking if God loved me, I should have been asking, *Do I love God?* His Word said that He loved me with an everlasting love, that He had plans to prosper and not to harm me, plans to give me a future and a hope. But Jesus also said, "If you love me, keep my commandments" (John 14:15). What I came to understand is that my victim mentality had led me to a place where I was not keeping His commandments or trusting in His Word. I did not believe the promises it contained; therefore, I was the one not loving Him, not the other way around.

When I understood this truth, I found such freedom. I didn't have to win God's affection; He already loved me! I could count on it because His Word said so, regardless of whether I felt it all the time. I realized that I am somebody to Him, somebody for whom He would die upon a cross. I began focusing on making sure God was somebody to me.

You see, we get it all wrong when it comes to how we think God thinks about us. We tend to think that God can only work with perfection. He is, after all, perfect. And we clearly are not. But the truth is just the opposite: it is God's strength that is made perfect through our weakness. The apostle Paul had a physical ailment of some sort. Some have suggested that he had an issue with his eyes, while others think it may have been a chronic painful condition that made his daily life challenging. Whatever it was, Paul struggled to see God working it all for good, until he acquired God's perspective on his weakened condition:

> Three different times I begged the Lord to take it away. Each time he said, "My grace is all you need. My power works best in weakness." So now I am glad to boast about my weaknesses, so that the power of Christ can work through me. That's why I take pleasure in my weaknesses, and in the insults, hardships, persecutions, and troubles that I suffer for Christ. For when I am weak, then I am strong (2 Corinthians 12:8-10 NLT).

How counterintuitive is that! God's power works best in our weakness? Some translations say that his strength is "made perfect" or "complete" in our weakness, as if God is at His best when working through our frail efforts. Perhaps that is why Paul later says, "If I must boast, I would rather boast about the things that show how weak I am." So do you think you are weak? Terrific! You are the most qualified person to show God to be strong. God delights in lifting the nobody to show that he or she is somebody to Him.

James affirms this thought but also offers a warning to those who think they are somebody because of their own efforts: "God opposes the proud but shows favor to the humble" (James 4:6). God lifts those who are willing to humble themselves and acknowledge their weakness, but He actively pushes back on those who think they do not need Him. Our pride can kill our chance at a better life when, like Nebuchadnezzar, a king of ancient Babylon, we take credit for God's goodness to us:

> "[King Nebuchadnezzar] was taking a walk on the flat roof of the royal palace in Babylon. As he looked out across the city, he said, 'Look at this great city of Babylon! By my own mighty power, I have built this beautiful city as my royal residence to display my majestic splendor.'
>
> "While these words were still in his mouth, a voice called down from heaven, 'O King Nebuchadnezzar, this message is for you! You are no longer ruler of this kingdom. You will be driven from human society. You will live in the fields with the wild animals, and you will eat grass like a cow. Seven periods of time will pass while you live this way, until you learn that the Most High rules over the kingdoms of the world and gives them to anyone he chooses.'
>
> "That same hour the judgment was fulfilled, and Nebuchadnezzar was driven from human society. He ate grass like a cow, and he was drenched with the dew of heaven. He lived this way until his hair was as long as eagles' feathers and his nails were like birds' claws.

"After this time had passed, I, Nebuchadnezzar, looked up to heaven. My sanity returned, and I praised and worshiped the Most High and honored the one who lives forever.

His rule is everlasting,
    and his kingdom is eternal.
All the people of the earth
    are nothing compared to him.
He does as he pleases
    among the angels of heaven
    and among the people of the earth.
No one can stop him or say to him,
    'What do you mean by doing these things?'

"When my sanity returned to me, so did my honor and glory and kingdom. My advisers and nobles sought me out, and I was restored as head of my kingdom, with even greater honor than before.

"Now I, Nebuchadnezzar, praise and glorify and honor the King of heaven. All his acts are just and true, and he is able to humble the proud" (Daniel 4:29-37 NLT).

God humbled the proud king who thought he was somebody apart from God. Yet it is also pride that causes us to think we are nobody when God says we are somebody to Him—as if we know better than He does. And sometimes our thinking can go so off course that we actually think *both* things are true about us *at the same time*—we are nobody *and* we deserve everything because of it. I guess, when it comes right down to it, we'll take any excuse to play the role of victim.

I used to think I knew my own worth better than God did. But I was wrong. Like John the Baptist who came to pave the way for

Jesus, my goal now is to decrease so that He may increase. I choose not to be a victim. I choose not to hide behind labels. I rest in the confidence that I have inestimable worth because God believes I am somebody no matter what I may feel.

If I Leave You as a Victim

Over the next seven chapters, I'm going to share with you a pathway to a better life, one where you can find the strength to deal with whatever problems you may face. Along the way, I may say some pretty direct stuff. You might even be offended by some of it. That's not my intention, but know this: I speak the truth because I genuinely care about people, and I believe God has something better for you. If I leave you as a victim of learned helplessness and tell you it's okay to be a victim, I'm saying there's no hope for you. And that's just not true.

If I truly care about you, I'm going to tell you some things that might rub you the wrong way. It's what Coach did for me so many years ago. The apostle Paul said that we "grow up" in Christ by "speaking the truth in love" to one another (Ephesians 4:15). So whatever you may read in the pages to come, know that it comes from a place of love and deep concern for all who are hurting and feel hopeless to do anything about it.

William Wilberforce was a man of great courage who said some pretty unwelcome things in his day. A few centuries ago, he tirelessly fought to end the wicked slave trade at the heart of England's economic system. When well-meaning friends advised him to quiet down, here's what he said: "If you love someone who is ruining his or her life because of faulty thinking, and you don't do anything about it because you are afraid of what others might think, it would seem that rather than being loving, you are in fact being heartless."[10] Our culture tells us that tolerance of everything is the way to go.

But I agree with Wilberforce. There are times when saying nothing would be heartless. And this is one of those times.

Jesus was a truth teller too. He never left anyone as a victim. He confronted even the Pharisees and Sadducees—the ones who harassed Him the most and eventually caused His crucifixion. He bluntly told them they had embraced a Satanic message: "You belong to your father, the devil, and you want to carry out your father's desires" (John 8:44). I mean, how do you say that in a nice way? But do you know why He told them that? It wasn't because He hated them, but because He loved them. He refused to leave them in that elitist state where they thought they were somebody apart from God. He saw the destruction headed their way and told them what they needed to hear. Because He loved them.

If I leave you as a victim, I don't love you. Some people tell me, "I am the way I am because of what my mom did to me." To that I say, "I get that when you were just a kid, but you're thirty years old. Come on! Quit being a victim of what happened to you when you were five. With God's help, you can grow and develop out of it."

God has given us the reasons to change. He's given us the power to change. And yet some people, even leaders in God's church, choose to say, "Well, there are mitigating circumstances." To that I say, "Then you don't believe the Bible. You have a form of godliness but you deny the very power of God to change our lives. And if I believed that, I wouldn't be where I am today." How great is your God anyway? My God, the God revealed in the Bible, is bigger than any problem I could ever face. What can't He do?

As I see it, we can choose either to wear our issues on our sleeves or to take them off. I know people who've been sexually abused who wear what happened to them for all to see. It becomes the label that defines who they are. On the other hand, I know people who've been sexually abused, but you would never know it now. It never affects them, because they don't wear it. So why, after thirty years, are some people still a victim of that one thing?

Yes, the abuse is horrific. Yes, what was done to them was terribly wrong. But at some point, people have to choose not to wear the label anymore. They must choose to say, "It happened. I can't have a do-over. But by God's strength, I'm going to take that label off. I'm not going to let it destroy me. I'm going to get help instead. I'm going to work through it and get it out of my life."

To those who hold on to hurts and victimhood labels, I understand why you think like that. Truly I do. But you can do better, be better, and live a better life. After all, that is the message of the gospel, isn't it? In Romans 1, the apostle Paul says that the good news of hope in Christ is the "power of God" applied to our sinful condition. What more could we ask for? What more could we need?

So enough with the excuses! Enough with the labels! Jesus didn't accept them and neither should we.

I love the story of what happened when Jesus encountered the man who'd been paralyzed for thirty-eight years. We might think that if anyone deserved to play the victim card, it would have been that guy. But Jesus did not agree. Some people apparently believed that, from time to time, an angel would stir up the waters of the pool and that the first person into the pool after each stirring would be healed. Don't ask me how it happened, but that is where Jesus met this man. The apostle John records what happened next:

> One who was there had been an invalid for thirty-eight years. When Jesus saw him lying there and learned that he had been in this condition for a long time, he asked him, "Do you want to get well?"
>
> "Sir," the invalid replied, "I have no one to help me into the pool when the water is stirred. While I am trying to get in, someone else goes down ahead of me."

> Then Jesus said to him, "Get up! Pick up your mat and
> walk." At once the man was cured; he picked up his mat
> and walked (John 5:5-9).

What I find amazing about this story is not that Jesus healed someone. He did that a lot. Jesus says two things to the man that blow me away. First, He asks the man a question: "Do you want to get well?" Now why would He ask that question after thirty-eight years—unless Jesus perceived that the man had already given up hope of being healed.

The truth is that God is often more willing to solve our problems than we are willing for Him to solve them. We get comfortable with our problems and good at offering excuses for them. In fact, the man's response suggests that he had already given up hope, for he doesn't say, "Of course I want to be healed! Can you help me?" Instead he offers an excuse, an explanation for why he is a victim of his circumstances: "I have no one to help me into the pool."

What Jesus does not say next is the message many victims hear today: "I feel your pain, man. Let me sit down next to you and commiserate with you about your struggle. Maybe we can start a protest or demand better care for people facing your problems in life."

Quite the contrary, in response to the man's excuse, Jesus says the second surprising thing: "Get up!" Essentially, Jesus was saying to the man, "Seriously? That's no excuse. You can be healed of your pain if you believe in Me. So get up and walk. Your sins are forgiven."

Amazing things happen when we believe the truth of God's Word, when we don't just agree with it, but act on it. I know a man who spent forty years in and out of prison as a heroin addict. Then one day someone came alongside and spoke the truth to him. "You can be different. You don't have to live this way. If you believe in God and work hard and act on this Word that's living and powerful, you can be free. You don't have to think like a victim anymore." Today if you were to see him, you would say there's no way that he had once struggled with such problems. But he did. And the best part is that he is now on staff here at Legacy Church and serving as a pastor.

Another man I know lost his job, so he began to panhandle in some of the grocery store parking lots in our community. After he gave his life to Christ, God began to challenge him to make some changes in his life. He said that he felt convicted about how he was treating people and money. He worked on being courteous and kind to others, and—get this—he began to tithe, to give 10 percent of all the money from panhandling to God. I've known professing Christians with great jobs and big salaries who refuse to tithe. This man, however, began to put God first in the midst of his dire circumstances. Before long, his faithfulness and his willingness to obey the Lord was rewarded as he found a full-time job that allowed him to find an apartment of his own.

When we encounter hope and follow His direction, we leave our victim status behind. Think of what Jesus said to the woman who was dragged before Him after being caught committing adultery. "Go now and leave your life of sin" (John 8:11). Real life-change. Mercy in the hour of greatest need. Truth to guide her into a new life.

Think of Zacchaeus, the guy who climbed the sycamore tree to catch a glimpse of Jesus. He got more than that when Jesus invited himself over to eat with him. And the end result? Zacchaeus went from being a thief and a liar to being an honest and generous man. Jesus didn't leave him in his sinful ways, and He won't leave you there either. If you follow God and act on His Word, you can and will change no matter what has happened to you in the past.

As Henry Malone, founder of Vision Life Ministries, once wisely said, "None of us are as free as Jesus died for us to be." God is always ready and eager to help, but we have to do our part. When we do what God says, God does what He says. It doesn't matter what labels we've had slapped on us in life, or what victim status we've given ourselves. He is the God of another chance, and your next chance starts right now.

WHAT YOU CAN DO NOW

- What labels have you allowed the enemy to put on you, whether through your own words and actions or those of others? Before you say none, seriously consider your answer. A label doesn't have to be shocking. Maybe it sounds like something good, such as "self-sufficient," but even that doesn't ring true for believers. We need God and other believers; we're not self-sufficient. So what labels have you allowed to be put on your life?

- Are you willing to allow God to remove those labels even if it takes work on your part? Even if it's uncomfortable or awkward? If you are, ask Him to direct you to the promises in His Word that contradict those labels. Then believe (don't just agree with) His promises. When you start to believe God about who you are, it becomes much easier to disbelieve the lies that Satan tells you about yourself.

- Evaluate where you play the victim card in your life. Is it at work? In a relationship? Wherever you find it, write it down on a piece of paper. Now hand it over to God. You don't want it, and He wants to get rid of it for you. Encounter God and leave the victim status behind.

Part 2

A PATHWAY
TO A BETTER LIFE

6

GET REAL
ABOUT YOUR LIFE

I t's not often that a pastor has nothing to say. But pain has a way of making us be quiet. Real life can really hurt. One day, it left me speechless.

We first met Tonja and Norman when we were pastoring in Roswell, New Mexico. Tonja came to my office one day with her infant son, who had cystic fibrosis. The doctors had cut him open and put him back together just so he could live. She sat on my office floor with me and my wife, opened up the blanket, and showed us her baby. She was devastated at all they had endured; our hearts broke for them.

"My husband just got a job and we don't have any money," she said. "Is there any way you can help us get to Albuquerque for my son's next doctor appointment?" Our church didn't have any money (in fact, our bank account balance was negative five hundred), but we rallied support and got some money together for her.

Over the next few years, Tonya and Norman became part of our church, along with their son and beautiful six-year-old daughter, who loved my wife. It was on my wife's birthday that we got a panicked call from a nurse.

"Tonja's on her way to the hospital," she told me. "Don't say a word to her, but you need to meet her there. She's been in a motorcycle accident."

"I'm on my way, but what am I not supposed to tell her?"

Their six-year-old daughter, healthy as could be, had died in the accident.

We went to the hospital and prayed for Tonja before she went into surgery. When her husband showed up later, the hospital staff escorted Norman and I to a private room. I remember thinking, *I don't know what to say*. He wept and all I could do was cry with him.

"What am I going to do?" he asked me.

"Norman, I have no words."

And we just wept some more. The pain my wife and I felt was intense, but it was nothing compared to their pain.

A few days later, we walked into the funeral home room where they had placed his little girl. Norman just fell to the floor in the middle of the room and wept. I will never forget it. I remember thinking, *How will they keep serving the Lord? Will they stay together?* I had never seen that type of pain. But they did stay together. And to this day they are still serving the Lord.

Not that it has been easy for them. Not that the road ahead will be easy for you, but no matter what you are going through, there is help and hope in Christ. Your heart may have been broken. Someone you love may have died or walked out of your life. You may have been abused as a child or even as an adult. You may have been rejected by your parents or even abandoned by those you trusted to always be there. You may feel overwhelmed and scared about the future.

Pain is real. It's not healthy to deny it. Part of getting real about our life is being honest with ourselves about the pain we've experienced. But once we are honest about it, we get to choose how we respond to it. No one can take that away from us.

Tonja and Norman could have given up and blamed God; but they chose to trust Him for the strength to keep moving forward. Some people teach that if you have faith in God, you won't have pain or troubles. They preach that if you trust God, you won't have any problems. Not true. Sometimes the pain can be so great that it takes faith just to wake up, eat a bowl of oatmeal, and go to work in the morning.

No matter where you are today, you can be assured that God, by His Holy Spirit, is there to help you one day at a time, one moment at a time. You will recover as you continue to trust Him and do as He asks. You see, Jesus came to heal the brokenhearted, to bind up our wounds, and to set us free from hurts that keep us captive (Luke 4:18). You don't have to allow your pain to turn into suffering that never heals. You can choose an expiration date for the hold that hurt has over you. You can choose a different path, a hopeful path, God's path for a better life.

Jesus Knows Pain

We all experience pain, whether physical or emotional. Physical pain can be as simple as a paper cut or stubbing your toe to something more challenging, like a broken bone or a disease or illness. I have cracked my collarbone and ribs, twisted my knee, hurt my back, and tweaked my ankle many times. For the most part, our bodies can and do heal after physical pain strikes.

My greatest pain has been emotional. At times I've felt sucker punched, as if life just snuck up and knocked the breath out of me. I've been sad, scared, and afraid of the unknown. I've experienced hurt. Emotional pain produces other problems in us: fear, discouragement, disappointment, bitterness, grief, disillusionment, hopelessness, and lethargy. Some handle emotional pain better than others. Some only mask it and tell themselves, "I'm OK." They may blame others, drink too much, take drugs, or seek comfort in promiscuous sex just to feel better for a moment. Because the temporary relief never lasts, they feel as if they have to indulge more every time. It can become a vicious cycle of despair.

God has healed me from my emotional pain, even though it was real and devastating at the time. I knew there was no other way but God's way, so walking away was never an option. I kept healing a little more every day, continuing to serve God while trusting in His Word.

Here's the good news: no matter what your pain, Jesus came to heal it all. Jesus said He was the Someone who'd been promised, the one who would bring rest, healing, and renewal to those in pain:

> "The Spirit of the Lord is upon Me,
> Because He has anointed Me
> To preach the gospel to the poor;
> He has sent Me to heal the brokenhearted,
> To proclaim liberty to the captives
> And recovery of sight to the blind,
> To set at liberty those who are oppressed."
> (Luke 4:18 NKJV)

I love how the Amplified Bible describes it: "He has sent Me...*to send forth as delivered* those who are oppressed [who are downtrodden, bruised, crushed, and broken down by calamity]." Jesus came to deliver us from the hold that painful circumstances can have over us. Even though calamity may have broken us down, He empowers us to set an expiration date for our pain.

Right now your pain may be all too real, your suffering so fresh your soul still bleeds as you read. But that doesn't mean you have to sorrow as if you had no hope. Hope has arrived, and He knows what it feels like to hurt. He endured the horrific physical pain of a crucifixion, the most painful form of death the Romans could inflict upon a person. He knows what it's like to be rejected by just about everyone, to watch His disciples abandon Him in His hour of greatest need. He knows what it feels like to have His heavenly Father turn His back as He took on Himself the sins of the world.

Jesus wept at the grave of a dear friend. He lived and walked alongside humanity in this real world, the one you and I live in each day. The writer of Hebrews tells us Jesus has been touched by our pain, He can "empathize with our weaknesses," because He "has been tempted in every way, just as we are—yet he did not sin" (Hebrews 4:15). The prophet Isaiah accurately foretold this painful version of Jesus's life on earth:

> He was despised and rejected by mankind,
>   a man of suffering, and familiar with pain.
> Like one from whom people hide their faces
>   he was despised, and we held him in low esteem.
> Surely he took up our pain
>   and bore our suffering,
> yet we considered him punished by God,
>   stricken by him, and afflicted.
> But he was pierced for our transgressions,
>   he was crushed for our iniquities;
> the punishment that brought us peace was on him,
>   and by his wounds we are healed.
>   (Isaiah 53:3-5)

Jesus knows pain. He knows your pain. That's why He extends this invitation to you:

"Come to me, all you who are weary and burdened, and I will give you rest. Take my yoke upon you and learn from me, for I am gentle and humble in heart, and you will find rest for your souls. For my yoke is easy and my burden is light" (Mathew 11:28-30).

Jesus isn't saying you should ignore your pain or pretend it doesn't exist. I'm not telling you your pain isn't real; just the opposite. I'm saying Jesus came to empower you to move forward to a better life in Him in spite of that pain. Your pain doesn't have to define you for the rest of your life and give you an excuse to quit. You may tell yourself, *I started drinking when this happened, so that's why I drink.* My friend, that may have been why you started, but it's time to put an expiration date on that pain. It's time to stop hurting yourself. It's time to stop self-sabotaging your future by letting a painful circumstance define your whole being.

You may have experienced real pain in your life, but what does God say? He said He came to heal the brokenhearted. If brokenhearted describes you, then it's time to take the first step. Start by humbling yourself and saying, *God, whatever that first step may be, I'll do it! If it means throwing away some bottles or flushing some pills, I'll do it. If it means picking up the phone to get help for my marriage, I'll do it. If it means breaking off a relationship that isn't helping, I'll do it.*

Go ahead and pause right now. Ask God to make the next step clear to you based on your unique circumstances. If you can't figure it out, talk to your pastor; call someone you know who loves God and His Word and ask them to speak the truth to you. Then commit to doing what God wants you to do next. Just do it. God can find you moving better than He can find you sitting still.

Does Jesus Care about Your Pain?

Sometimes we may wonder if Jesus cares about our suffering. The Bible says Jesus was, again and again, moved with compassion for the hurting. Compassion is different from sympathy. Sympathy feels sorry for someone, but compassion happens when we share the person's pain in a way that moves us to act.

Throughout the biblical accounts of His life, we find Jesus overflowing with compassion that moved Him to take action:

- "When Jesus landed and saw a large crowd, he had compassion on them and healed their sick" (Matthew 14:14).

- "Moved with compassion, Jesus reached out and touched [a man with leprosy]" (Mark 1:41 NLT).

- "When he saw the crowds, he had compassion on them, because they were harassed and helpless, like sheep without a shepherd" (Matthew 9:36).

- "Jesus called his disciples to him and said, 'I have compassion for these people...I do not want to send them away hungry, or they may collapse on the way'" (Matthew 15:32).

- "Jesus had compassion on [the blind men] and touched their eyes. Immediately they received their sight and followed him" (Matthew 20:34).

- "A dead person was being carried out—the only son of his mother, and she was a widow...When the Lord saw her, his heart went out to her and he said, 'Don't cry.'...He said, 'Young man, I say to you, get up!' The dead man sat up and began to talk, and Jesus gave him back to his mother" (Luke 7:12-15).

Finding the Source

If we're going to get real about our lives, we need to identify the source of our problems. Our pain can come from three main sources. Although God remains our hope for dealing with all three types, each one requires a different approach, either in ourselves or in others.

External Pain

In this fallen world, horrific things happen. We don't have to ask for problems. We don't have to do anything to cause them. Sometimes tragedy strikes and we're left to pick up the pieces.

I recall watching an episode of the television show *The Biggest Loser* many years ago that exemplified this kind of pain. For those not familiar with the show, it tells the stories of people who are overweight—often extremely overweight—and follows their efforts to lose weight. The episode that made such an impression on me featured a woman who had once been happily married with children—a beautiful family. One day her husband and kids went to the store and never returned. They were all struck by a car and killed. In an instant, she lost her entire family. Man, let me tell you, everybody on the show was crying. She said she had just wanted to quit living, so she used to stay home and eat. She had tried to find comfort from the unbelievably intense external pain through food, but it had only made her life worse.

And if you ever watch that show, almost all the participants have had a similar experience. Something devastating took place and they responded in a similar way. There's always an underlying cause, but if you have experienced external pain, there is hope for you in Jesus.

Self-Induced Pain

Sometimes the pain we feel is the result of our own mistakes. We may not like admitting it, but we begin to find healing only when we acknowledge we were wrong. We can't get help until we acknowledge we have a problem that we helped to cause.

Several years ago I met with a lady and her husband who wanted to serve in our church. To protect all the children here at Legacy, we require a background check for all members. She told me that she was not usually a drinker, but she had been out one night and had some drinks. As she was driving home, she rear-ended another car and killed someone—a child.

I just looked at her, stunned by her admission. But she said she knew she had messed up. Both she and her husband made it clear that she had made a terrible mistake. They told me the case was going through the courts, but they still wanted to serve at church in some way because they wanted to be plugged in to a church community. She couldn't undo the horrible mistake she had made, but she took responsibility for her life going forward. She did end up going to prison as a consequence of her mistake. But seven years later, she now works at the church and her husband is a leader here as well.

Mistakes do not need to end our lives, no matter how much they may hurt. We must acknowledge our responsibility in creating self-induced pain and believe that Jesus loves us and offers hope for a better life in spite of the problems we've created for ourselves.

Prosperity Pain

I mentioned this pain earlier in our journey, but it's worth revisiting briefly here. The truth is that for most of us, we only think we're in pain. We think we are suffering or that God is out to get us simply because we don't get what we want. It's a problem unique to wealthy nations such as ours. In countless nations around the globe, people have to trust God today just to find food to eat. If we compared our list of pains to those of a starving child, we'd find our-list doesn't really compare. If we had to trust in God every day to eat, we wouldn't have time to deal with trivial disappointments. We wouldn't have time to be depressed. Most of our pains are about what we don't get or what doesn't go our way.

We blame God for it because that's what the world has taught us to do. Somehow it's God's fault, because if He really loved us, He would give us what we want. Think about what we're saying when we embrace that mindset. We say, "I blame God because He didn't give me the job I wanted." When did God become your genie in a bottle? Maybe He didn't want you to have that job because He knew it wasn't the best for you. Here's a crazy thought: maybe you don't have the job because you weren't qualified for it, or you weren't willing to go back to school, or you weren't willing to learn and grow anymore.

Why is it God's fault when we don't get what we want? We celebrate Him when we get everything we want, and we hate Him when we don't. Really? So He's not the Lord of all of life, just the parts we like. But that's not total surrender.

We have it so good, and still we whine and complain about what we want. God promises to give us what we need, not what we want. And most people in America have very few needs. They have a place to live. They have clothes. They have food on the table. Almost everybody has those needs met. If we compare our discomfort to Iraqi Christians who must trust God to preserve their lives, we've got it pretty good. John Eldredge said, "When we believe we need whatever is just beyond our reach, we are miserable."

What's in Your Scotoma?

Have you ever lost your car keys? It's funny how many times I've told my wife, "Honey, I can't find my car keys," and then she walks over and says, "They're right here in front of you." Well, it's funny now, but not so much when it happens.

How in the world could something be right in front of me and I not see it? Well, it's actually quite easy. Our brains are always trying to convince us that we are in balance, that we are sane and rational people. So if I say, "I cannot find my car keys," my brain takes the necessary steps to convince me that I am correct in thinking that I am incapable of finding my car keys. So I just don't see them. They could be sitting right in front of me on my desk, but I won't see them because I can't. Or so I've told myself.

The technical name for this phenomenon is a *scotoma*, but most people call it by a more common name—a blind spot. And we've all got 'em, both in our physical eyes and in our perspective on our problems. There are things in each of our lives that we have convinced ourselves to be true—or untrue—and we block out anything that might contradict that conclusion.

So if we believe that God is out to get us, we will fail to see how much He is blessing us even though He may be pouring bucket after bucket of blessings on us. We could be the most blessed person on the planet and still whine and complain that God doesn't love us. We've got a massive blind spot warping our perspective. If we embrace a victim mentality, then we can't take responsibility for anything—that would just make us seem crazy. It can't be our fault; after all, we're helpless victims.

The funny thing about blind spots is that we are almost always the last person to know we have one. Nothing is out of place from our point of view because we cannot see what is wrong—even if everyone else can. Blind spots can also cause us to get so used to a certain behavior that we don't even see it as destructive, as self-sabotaging the better life we supposedly want. When that happens, we usually can't get real about our lives until pain gets our attention or someone loves us enough to confront us and slap us back into reality.

Many years ago I was visiting a pastor friend of mine, and we dropped in on worship practice. My friend stopped the entire rehearsal and had everyone take a seat. I sat down to one side, wondering what he was going to do. It didn't take long to find out, unfortunately. He began walking around the group, and then suddenly he stopped and confronted one guy.

"You. Did you know so-and-so was sick?"

And I'm thinking, *Oh, my gosh. Where is this going?*

"Well, yeah," the guy replied.

"Did you call him?"

I began shrinking a little bit in my seat.

"Well, no."

"You didn't call him because you didn't care."

I was mortified. And then my friend went to someone else and started in again, accusing someone else of not caring. He proceeded to go around the group, exposing what he perceived to be shortcomings in their ministry. I remember feeling so awkward and thinking, *I hope they don't think I would do this.*

Once the inquisition was over, my friend and I went to a conference together. He brought up what happened at the worship practice and invited my input.

"Listen, I'm open," he said. "Tell me anything you want."

"No, I'm not going to do this," I said. "You have a good night."

"No, tell me. You didn't like what I did?"

"Look, when we're done, you're not going to like me."

But he swore he wouldn't get mad at me and said, "I need you to talk to me."

So, I just laid it all out there. "What you did was so wrong. If I were in your church, I would have never come back. I would never serve with you. I thought we were servants, man. I know you were sincere, but you treated those people so mean. It's pathetic leadership. It's bad. You put those people on the spot. You ridiculed them in front of their peers. Over what? They didn't call somebody? They're obviously already serving at the church, getting ready to lead worship. As I sat there listening to you, my heart was sinking, and I was thinking, 'How can I run out of here, because I don't want these people to think I'm like you.'"

No doubt about it, I was rough on him. Do you know why? He had no idea what he had done.

He looked at me stunned and asked, "Did I do that?"

"Absolutely, you did that!"

When I left the room that night, I presumed our relationship was over. No matter what promises he had made, I was pretty sure that our friendship was done. The next morning as I was eating breakfast, he found me and sat down next to me.

"I've got to tell you something," he said.

I thought, *Yep, just as I expected. Here it comes.*

"Do you know what I did last night? I called every member of my staff. I called my leaders, and I repented to each and every one."

I stopped eating so I wouldn't choke.

"I told them I had acted like this, and you know what every one of them said? 'Yeah, you do that a lot.' I repented all night long, and I gave them my word, 'I will never treat you like that again.'"

See, he didn't know! He's a wonderful guy, a good-hearted man who loves people. He just had a blind spot the size of New Mexico.

Just a Thought:
Find Your Blind Spots

Blind spots are just that—blind to us but not to everyone else. Find a trusted friend or mentor and be willing
to have the tough conversation and ask the tough questions. It doesn't mean they will be 100 percent correct. But
if they care about you, they can help you identify what
might be hindering you from reaching your goal. For
example, maybe you tend to be moody. If you are having a bad day, you should be the only one who knows
it. You can take control over your mood if that is what's
holding you back. Just a thought...

Get Real to Get Better

You can't get to a better place in life until you get real about your
life. That means getting realistic about your problems. As I said in
chapter 2, your problem isn't the problem. It's your perspective on
the problem that will determine your success going forward. Until
you are ready to get real about the role you may have played in causing your pain—or perceived prosperity pain—you can't begin to
grow and change.

On the other hand, you may have suffered real pain, external
pain that has left you gasping for air. My friend, please hear me: I'm
not saying you're not hurting. Not at all. What I am saying is that
you can live with that pain the rest of your life or you can begin to
take steps toward a better life.

My dad was only sixty-six when he died. The doctor had said the
day before my dad died that he would be released from the hospital

the next day. At first, I was completely heartbroken because I loved him so much. My dad was my hero. I still miss him, but I don't feel the pain. Don't get me wrong. There are times when I think, *I wish he were around. I wish he could see what God has done.* But the pain doesn't cripple me anymore. I had to decide not to stay in that painful place. I chose an expiration date for my pain and began to move forward.

The pathway ahead is not a magical formula that makes pain and problems disappear. That's not what it's about. It's about recognizing that God is bigger than any problem you face, any pain you encounter. It's about a commitment to obey His Word and trust in Him. As you do that, He will heal your pain and insecurities just as He promised. He will make all things new. It might happen quickly for some but take more time for others. Your journey is uniquely your journey.

Norman and Tonja's journey continued after they pressed on past the pain of their daughter's death. In the years that followed, we moved to Albuquerque and they moved to Mississippi. But we still kept in touch. Last year, Norman texted me out of the blue with more tragic news. Their son, that baby we had met on the floor in my office nineteen years earlier, had just taken his own life.

Cystic fibrosis had been a death sentence from the beginning; he wasn't supposed to have lived past fifteen or sixteen. Every few months he had to go in and have his lungs cleaned out. He could never take a deep breath. When he'd left the hospital the last time, he told his parents, "I'm never going back to the hospital." They didn't think much of it until he was due to go back again, but took his life instead. All over again, this couple was devastated, and once again, I didn't know what to say.

Today, in spite of the pain they've experienced and the problems they've faced, Norman and Tonja are still attending church and serving God faithfully. Just to be candid, I don't know if I could have done that. I hope so, but clearly God's grace is at work in their lives. I know they must have wanted to give up, but they kept moving forward. Author and speaker Nido Qubein states this basic truth that my friends so powerfully live: "Your present circumstances don't dictate where you can go. They merely determine where you start."

WHAT YOU CAN DO NOW

- Take a mental inventory of some of the most painful times in your life—physical, emotional, mental. How did you react to the pain? Look for a pattern (anger, seclusion, destructive behavior), and avoid the instinct to react that way in the future. If you've already developed the healthy habit of turning to God in your pain, then by all means, keep on turning.

- If you don't see a pattern, ask someone you trust to lovingly describe how you reacted in those situations. It could be that it's all in your blind spot.

- If you have learned to turn to God for help in your pain, start to reach out to others you may know who are in pain. Share the good news of hope in Christ. Minister to those you can help and pray for those you can't.

7

CHOOSE YOUR NEW DIRECTION

I sat in my office one day several years ago praying about the direction of our church. I sensed that we were bumping up against an invisible ceiling. We weren't facing some sort of disaster at the time, but my leadership senses were tingling. As I prayed, I couldn't escape this thought: If I kept doing what I was doing, kept leading the way I was leading, the church would never grow beyond where it was. I felt maxed out. I couldn't find a way to put more into my schedule.

As I prayed, I had another thought that I believe came from God: I either need to give away parts of the ministry and empower other people to do it or prepare for an early grave trying to do it all.

I made a decision that day to go in a new direction. I decided to focus on raising up leaders in the church, people to whom I could entrust parts of the ministry so I could focus on what I do best. I've got to tell you, it was a scary thing for me to let go of that control. But the church started growing again, because I was willing to change the way I function. You see, we have to make room for growth before we can have growth.

One problem I have with taking a new direction is one you may understand. I'm always talking about starting in a new direction *tomorrow* (in the land of mañana). For years I said I would get in shape and start working out regularly. I told my wife, "I'm going to start soon. Any day now, I'll get to it." But that day never quite seemed to arrive. Even though I had gotten real about my unhealthy situation, I hadn't yet chosen a new direction. I was still headed in the old direction—mostly a wider direction!

Finally the day arrived when I'd had enough. I told my wife, "Alright, Cynthia, I am starting today." And I did. Two and a half years later, I still work out consistently, nearly every day. I have never been in better physical shape even though I previously played sports and refereed for many years. But we're the greatest procrastinators aren't we? What we really need to do is to take our decisions out of the future and move them into the now. Only then can we begin to deal with the problems we identify when we get real about our lives.

What It Will Take to Change

I'm not trying to say that you can do this through willpower alone. The bookshelves are full of self-help books that sell you tips for trying harder or offer a better system for living a problem-free life. The airwaves are full of promises of a better life *if only* you'll make a donation to a cause or purchase mystical olive oil from the Promised Land. Don't waste your money on that stuff. Near election time, politicians promise a better life even though they really can't do much about it. The truth is that once you get real about the problems in your life, your next step to a better life is to intentionally choose a new direction.

It's been said that if you always do what you've always done, you'll always get what you've always gotten. If you want a better life, stuff has to change. You can't keep living the life you're living now and expect anything other than the results you've been getting. You must turn from the way you have been believing, thinking, and living and turn toward a deeper relationship with your Creator. You must surrender your will to the One who longs to make you the best version of you that you can be. Either that or live life your own way. You can't have it both ways. Jesus Himself said you're either for Him or against Him (Luke 11:23). That's pretty straightforward stuff. His Word must become the guiding light in our lives, even if that truth goes against what the world says.

God says in Isaiah 30:15 (AMP) that our hope lies in doing two things—returning and trusting: "For thus said the Lord God, the Holy One of Israel: In returning [to Me] and resting [in Me] you shall be saved; in quietness and in [trusting] confidence shall be your strength." God calls us to change our direction and trust in His promises. Some translations use the word *repentance* here instead of *returning.* God is calling us to believe and to repent.

Repent is not a popular word in these days when we tolerate everyone and everything. But repentance begins with recognizing that God is right and I am wrong. Repentance says to God, "I'm willing to stop doing what I am doing and start doing what's right in Your sight."

For example, the Bible says, "Each of you must put off falsehood and speak truthfully to your neighbor" (Ephesians 4:25). Stop lying and tell the truth. So when is a liar no longer a liar according to this verse? It's not just when he's not lying; it's when he has changed direction by speaking the truth instead, because his heart has been realigned with God's.

The Bible is full of this call to pursue a new direction in Christ. When Peter preached of God's deliverance, the people pleaded to know what they must do to be saved from their destructive ways. He said they must do two things: repent and be baptized (Acts 2:38). We must turn away from the self-sabotaging life and turn instead toward the Giver of abundant life. Oh, and join a church, he says.

That's essentially what Peter is saying when he says to be baptized. There are a lot of other theological implications, but when it comes right down to it, Peter is telling them to get connected with others who share that commitment to new life in Christ. We'll circle back to the importance of a local church a little later, but we first must turn away from our own sinful and destructive desires.

The Bible describes us as being in bondage to those desires. We need to hear the truth about sin so we know we have a choice to change. Young people are deceived into accepting certain lifestyles because no one tells them the truth. No one says it is wrong. Many people are surprised to learn how many homosexuals attend Legacy Church while trying to find freedom from that lifestyle. You might think they would hate me for speaking the truth to them, but you know what they say? "At least you cared enough to tell the truth. Unless I'd heard what God says about sexual immorality, I would never have known. Everybody else told me it's just the way God made me. But when I come to Legacy, I hear, 'God didn't make you that way. You may be predisposed to certain temptations, but it doesn't mean you have to live it.'"

Today we blur the lines and tolerate everything. Either we're to accept it all or be labeled as intolerant. Frankly, I don't care how people label me; I only care how God labels me. If I listen to what the world tells me, truth is the new hate speech. If I speak truth today, even to some Christians, they freak out. They tell me, "That's a little too strong or too tough." But political correctness is just another word for cowardice. It isn't only robbing us of freedom of speech in America; it's eliminating our access to the truth. And without truth, we have no hope of ever finding a better life.

Those who preach political correctness want me to say, "I don't believe in anything." In our culture today, if you believe in something, you're labeled a radical. If we choose to follow the Word of God, we're radicals. If we call homosexual behavior a sin, as God does in His Word, we're extremists. No matter how many times I read the Bible, the word *fornication* means *any* sexual activity outside of marriage. My job is not to apologize for God or even to stand up for Him. He can stand on His own just fine without me. My job is to stand *with* God and say to all I encounter, "Because I love you, let me tell you what God says about the destructive effects of sin on our lives." I'm not going to make room for sin so someone else can feel better about choosing the wrong direction. And neither should you.

Just a Thought:
We Need a DNA Change

We all have predispositions. In my family, one of the predispositions was an addiction to alcohol. My grandfathers, my dad, my brothers, and I all struggled with it at some point. I worked hard to protect my children by telling them, "We have that predisposition in our family, so don't ever get started." But predisposition doesn't mean I have to be that way, and that truth applies to any area of life. God has set me free from those predispositions. We all have predispositions; we all need a DNA change. And the only way to get it is to ask Jesus to be Lord of our lives. When we do, we move from victim to conqueror as God works within us to overcome those destructive tendencies common to us all. Just a thought...

Making Room for Sin

When we make room for sin, we make room for evil and the enemy in our lives. It's as if we're moving over a little on the couch so sin can sit down and get cozy. The apostle Paul warns us of that very thing: "When angry, do not sin; do not ever let your wrath (your exasperation, your fury or indignation) last until the sun goes down. Leave no [such] room or foothold for the devil [give no opportunity to him]" (Ephesians 4:26-27 AMP). We give Satan an opening to divert us from our new direction when we don't chase after the truth and chase away sin.

When my son Stevie works with our youth at Legacy Church, he tells them the only way to get free of their problems is through spending time with God by reading His Word. They often respond, "Well, I don't really do that." So Stevie speaks the truth in love: "If you're not going to chase after truth, then I can't help you." Teenage girls tell him, "This guy treats me bad, but I just keep going back to him." When he tells them, "Change your phone number," they reply, "I don't really want to do that." What can he say then but, "If you don't want to run from trouble, not even God can help you." One girl he told me about had been saying for more than six months that she wanted to steer clear of harmful relationships; but she refused to change her phone number. She wanted to hold on to sinful influences and still get the benefits of choosing a new direction.

It doesn't work that way.

You see, we get comfortable with our sin. We adjust to it, just as our eyes adjust to different levels of darkness. When we make room for sin, we grow accustomed to the darkness. But the Bible says that if we hang out in the darkness, we won't find God there:

> God is light; in him there is no darkness at all. If we
> claim to have fellowship with him and yet walk in the

darkness, we lie and do not live out the truth. But if we walk in the light, as he is in the light, we have fellowship with one another, and the blood of Jesus, his Son, purifies us from all sin (1 John 1:5-7).

Oswald Chambers, author of *My Utmost for His Highest*, says, "It is perilously easy to have amazing sympathy with God's truth and remain in sin." I would add that if we continue to make room for sin, it spirals into a lifestyle of darkness that the Bible refers to as "iniquity."

There's a difference between iniquity and sin. *Sin* is any single thought, word, or deed that falls short or misses the mark of God's righteousness. *Iniquity* is a form of sin that runs deeper and refers to a life direction that is consistently off course. When we trust in Christ, His blood frees us from the power of sin, but that doesn't mean it's going to be easy to overcome all of it. Where sin is a one-time act, iniquity is more of a character flaw or a stronghold that must be dismantled through concentrated effort. Isaiah tells us Jesus "was pierced for our transgressions, he was crushed for our iniquities" (Isaiah 53:5). Solomon says, "By mercy and truth iniquity is purged: and by the fear of the LORD men depart from evil" (Proverbs 16:6 KJV).

Iniquity is more a habit of disobedience to God. It requires more than just a prayer to purge it from our lives. It takes proactive intervention. Left unchecked, it leads us down a road where we have no more fear of God in that area of our lives. Eventually, we get to the point where we say, "I've crossed so many lines that I don't care what God thinks, I'm going to do what I want." Then iniquity becomes part of our life. When that happens, we are on dangerous ground because we no longer even want to repent, to turn from sin and run to God.

Why "I'm Sorry" Doesn't Cut It

Repentance is more than expressing regret; it's more than just apologizing. It's not just me telling God, "Hey, I'm sorry I did that." We can apologize because we got caught, but that doesn't mean there's anything within us that says, "I'm going to work hard never to do that again." Repentance includes sorrow for our sin, but it also involves asking God's forgiveness and purposing in our hearts to never do it again. If I do it again, I repent again.

I think we've learned to apologize too much in our world today. We've learned to say we're sorry because that's politically correct. Real repentance produces a changed life.

When John the Baptist, the forerunner of Jesus, encountered sin, he just laid it out without holding anything back:

> But when [John] saw many of the Pharisees and Sadducees coming to where he was baptizing, he said to them: "You brood of vipers! Who warned you to flee from the coming wrath? Produce fruit in keeping with repentance. And do not begin to say to yourselves, 'We have Abraham as our father.' For I tell you that out of these stones God can raise up children for Abraham. The ax is already at the root of the trees, and every tree that does not produce good fruit will be cut down and thrown into the fire" (Matthew 3:7-10).

Wow! A pack of poisonous snakes! John didn't exactly take a page from *How to Win Friends and Influence People* when confronting the religious leaders. They thought God approved of them no matter how they lived. They were counting on their family heritage to cover their sinful actions. But God demands fruit as evidence of real heart change. If you've truly repented and chosen a new direction, prove it! Let's see the fruit.

If you were to plant some young fruit trees in your backyard and then invite me over, I'd ask, "What kind of tree is that one?" You'd check the label and tell me it's an apple tree. "What about that one over there?" You'd check that label. "Peach tree." Then, because I can be a real pain sometimes, I'd ask, "Are you sure? I don't see any fruit on them?" At that point, you'd roll your eyes and wish you hadn't invited me over before explaining, "That's because I just planted them! Come back in a few years and you'll see the fruit."

What John is saying in the passage above is that we've got to be able to take off the tag at some point and know the tree by the fruit it produces. There's got to be apples on a tree at some point to make it an apple tree. So it is with God. If you're going to repent and follow Him, your life must produce fruit that matches. True repentance produces real life-change. What we do reveals what's in our hearts.

Five Keys to Real Life-Change

True repentance produces real life-change. What we do reveals what's in our heart. I hear so many people today say, "You can't judge me, you don't know my heart." You're right. I don't know your heart. I don't know your intentions. But I do see your actions. Matthew 7:16 records Jesus saying we will know who is real "by their fruit." I can never judge your heart, but Jesus does call each of us to evaluate actions.

To experience growth, you must change what you do. Judge your own fruit. Try these five steps to real life-change:

1. *Be real.* You start where you are. It might not be a pretty place, but it's a start. It's not where you start but where you finish that's important.

2. *Be honest.* There's no point in pretending. You'll only

hurt your own growth. Don't sugarcoat your situation. Tell yourself the truth.

3. *Purpose to change.* Choose your new direction and make the choice to go there—no matter what.

4. *Realize God is not condemning you for where you are.* He is lovingly longing to lead and guide you into all truth.

5. *Start doing things God's way.* Real life-change happens when we choose to walk down a different street in order to arrive at a new destination.

Real Change Takes Time

When we truly choose a new direction, our actions will prove it—and the result will be a reinvigorated relationship with God, not just as Savior but as the loving Lord of our life who ensures that all things work together for our good. If we say we want a better life but we don't do what is required to live that life, we continue to self-sabotage our efforts. It's what happens over time that demonstrates the condition of our heart.

When I was nineteen, I went to church because a friend whose brother was the pastor had invited me. We had been out drinking the night before (true story) but staggered into the service that morning. For some reason I couldn't quite understand, I went back on Wednesday and again the next Sunday and even Sunday night. When they asked if anyone wanted to repent and turn to God, I raised my hand. Let me tell you, the greatest thing that ever happened to me was that someone said, "If you don't have Jesus, you're going to die and go to hell." So that's how I got saved.

And it changed me. I was born again through the Holy Spirit in me, but it freaked my brain out. I knew I needed to change the way

I lived, because it seemed as if everything I did was a sin. The way I thought, the way I talked, the way I acted—I was so overwhelmed. I didn't even know what sin was until I got saved, because it was just my normal life.

So when I trusted Christ, I saw my sin everywhere. I heard that I shouldn't misuse God's name, think dirty thoughts, or get drunk. I thought, *Oh, my gosh, that's most of my vocabulary. OK, I've got to change that. No dirty thoughts? Well, that's all I think about! No more getting drunk? Really?*

What I had to realize then is what you may need to realize now if you are overwhelmed at how much needs to change in your life. God is going to deal with issues in your life over time; when you overcome one, you'll have faith to overcome another. As C.S. Lewis put it in *Mere Christianity*, "Good and evil both increase at compound interest. That is why the little decisions you and I make every day are of such infinite importance."

Over time, your life will show significant fruit of your repentance. But it's going to take work. It's not just a one-time decision where you show up one day and you're done. It's going to take a lifetime of work in the real world.

It's a process for all of us. We've got to allow people, including ourselves, grace to falter and make mistakes as we walk forward in Christ. Sometimes people just need someone to say, "You can do better than this." If that's what you need, then know this: I believe that you can be better, do better, and live better by choosing a new direction in Christ. Not tomorrow or next week but today. Starting right now.

WHAT YOU CAN DO NOW

- Ask yourself this question and be honest in your response: "What sins have I made room for in my life? How are they hindering me from surrendering control and growing closer to God?" What sins, big or little, have you allowed to hang out on your couch and get cozy? If it helps to make a list, do it now. Then prayerfully take the first step to get rid of them.

- Be willing to seek accountability. One of Satan's most effective ploys is to isolate believers by making them think they're the only ones who struggle with sin. Don't let that be you! Find someone you trust and ask them to help by keeping you accountable for your actions or simply by praying for you to overcome something you're struggling with. Give them permission to ask for regular progress reports on the fruit your life is producing.

- Do you know someone who is struggling with sin? Be willing to hold your friend accountable for their walk with the Lord. Sometimes people have glaring flaws because no one *loves* them enough to gently point them out and keep them accountable. Love your brother (or sister) and encourage them through accountability.

8

THINK
NEW THOUGHTS

esearchers test some strange stuff, don't they? I came across a
study involving babies lying in a crib. Apparently, the researchers wanted to see if these babies could learn to be helpless. So they
created a special pillow on which a baby's head would lie that con-
trolled the hanging toy above them. They gave these special pillows
to half the babies in the study and gave regular pillows to the others.

Over time, the ones whose pillows could control the overhead
toy had a grand old time watching it move at their bidding. The
babies with normal pillows didn't discover any connection between
their actions and the overhead toy. But then the researchers did
something interesting. They switched pillows. The babies who origi-
nally couldn't control the overhead toy were now put into a position
where they could control the toy using the special pillows.

You'd think they'd get excited about their new ability, wouldn't
you? And yet, they did nothing with their new ability. They didn't
move the toy at all. In fact, they never even tried. This group had
learned that nothing they did would affect their environment, so
even though they could have easily moved on the new pillows to
control the toy, they did not even try. They had developed learned

helplessness. Because of their previous experiences, they did not think change was possible.

We can be a lot like those babies, can't we? We may have chosen an expiration date for our pain and a new direction in Christ, but that doesn't mean everything instantly changes. God's grace can fast-forward our story to a future filled with hope, but we can't delete scenes we regret from our lives. As we saw in the last chapter, we can still struggle mightily with sin. We can still function with a mindset of learned helplessness if that's all we've ever known.

Thank God that, because it was learned, helplessness can be unlearned. But like those babies in the research study, as long as we think that there is nothing we can do to change, then there *is* nothing we can do to change—because the way we think is everything.

The Highway to Our Minds

I've heard it said that words are tags for thoughts. If that's true, it's no wonder words can so radically change how we think. If eyes are the windows to the soul, then words are the highways to our minds.

Many of us allow ourselves to be held in bondage by words, sometimes even words that were said to us as children. If we're told long enough that we are no good, we may start to believe it. We then begin to tell ourselves, *I'm not smart enough. I'm not good enough. I could never do better or achieve that.*

Before we know it, those words begin to change the way we think about ourselves. This negative scripting soon produces negative thoughts that spiral downward into negative actions. Like the babies I mentioned earlier, we think life just is a certain way—even when it isn't true anymore.

Once we trust Christ, He frees us from the power of sin, but not the presence of sinful influences. He frees us from bondage to sin, but we must still take every thought captive, one by one. The apostle

Paul makes it sound like a mental war zone when he writes, "We demolish arguments and every pretension that sets itself up against the knowledge of God, and we take captive every thought to make it obedient to Christ" (2 Corinthians 10:5).

Although we no longer have to sin once we trust Christ to save us, we do have to go to war to get every thought under control. When I chose a new direction at the age of nineteen, I didn't get to go directly to heaven. I'll be there someday—thank God—but like you, I'm still living in a broken world where I've got work to do. And so do you.

Paul says we must subdue "every pretension that sets itself up against the knowledge of God." Notice first that we, and not God, are to take our thoughts captive. Of course, He is the one who strengthens us and works within us, but we are responsible to do what we need to do in order to get our thinking under control.

Second, what thoughts do we need to control? Any thought that doesn't line up with God's thoughts. God would never tell you that you are no good, so that thought has to go. He would never tell you that you are out of chances, so that thought must go. Anything that fails to pass the God test has to go.

Third, we can't be nice about getting rid of these thoughts. The language Paul uses here is military language. When someone is taken captive by military forces, they are corralled and put away so they can no longer fight or influence the war's outcome anymore. So it must be with our thoughts. We must ruthlessly seize ungodly thoughts, isolate them from our thought process, and throw away the key! Here's the reality: some of us are just too darn nice to thoughts we should be starving to death.

Albert Einstein, a guy who knew a little bit about thinking, said, "We cannot solve our problems with the same thinking we used when we created them."[11] Man, was he ever right. And when we submit to Christ's direction for our lives, our thoughts don't just need a new coat of paint; they need a complete renovation.

One of my favorite verses in the Bible says: "Do not conform to the pattern of this world, but be transformed by the renewing of your mind. Then you will be able to test and approve what God's will is—his good, pleasing and perfect will" (Romans 12:2). The word Paul uses here that is translated "renewing" doesn't refer to a weekend remodeling job. It describes a full-scale demolition—the kind where cabinets come down, walls get knocked down, and everything must go so it can be rebuilt the right way.

When I first came to Christ, I had a lot of negative thoughts I had picked up along the way. I used to think I wasn't good enough. I was really intimidated by people of authority. They didn't do anything to intimidate me; it was just how I thought about myself, and I couldn't talk to them at times. It was dumb. I would kick myself and wonder why I got so nervous. I had to renew my mind by the Word of God to think differently. I had to realize God created me and that I had great value to Him.

Another time, a necktie taught me I had to work to change prideful thinking. I had been giving a buddy of mine a hard time about a really sharp tie he was wearing. I said, "Hey, I'm believing God for a tie like that." I kept at it, half-jokingly. Finally, he just turned and offered me the tie. I said, "No, man, you know I'm playing. I don't want your tie." And then he said something to another person who was with us, something that changed my thinking in a moment. He said, "Steve's too proud to receive a gift."

Wow! It stopped me right there and made me think. I thought, *If I am too proud to accept gifts from people, I need to change my thinking.* I soon realized I had a false sense of humility; if someone told me, "Hey, you did a great job," I'd say, "Ah, man, no way." Why couldn't

I just say "Thank you" with humility? My thoughts were out of line with God's thoughts.

When we renew our minds, we align our thoughts with God's thoughts. We become more peaceful, happier, and more joyful; we begin to see our problems in a different light. It is so refreshing when we recognize the lies of the enemy, confront them, and replace them with truth from God. But I'm not saying it's easy. I understand what it is to have to work hard to renew your mind.

The Hard Work of Thinking New Thoughts

So many times I talk about changing and growing and people start whining. They say, "It's no fun. It's hard work." Yes, growth is hard work. Changing your thinking can be a tough process sometimes.

In my experience, most people think hard work is a disease—and they've built up an immunity to it. I hear them say, "If it's not easy, I don't want it." But anything worth having will take work. And here's what I find to be true of people: When they work for something, they appreciate it. When it's just given to them, they don't.

So when we have certain classes in our church—not all of them, but some—we require participants to pay for their own workbook. We discovered that if they pay something, even five dollars, they'll show up. But if we just give it to them, they'll often take advantage of it. In the same way, when we do the hard work of renewing our minds in Christ, we'll appreciate the end result.

Some people are surprised that I talk a lot about doing hard work to achieve a better life. They think that's not what pastors of large churches do, I guess. We once had a consulting group visit our church so we could get their counsel in a number of areas. After hearing me preach, one consultant told me he was surprised by what he heard. He said, "You preach a message that says 'Listen! This is life, this is how you walk it out, and these are the steps you've got to take.' I was fascinated because, given the diversity of your church, I would have bet you would be preaching a message like 'Your Miracle Is Tomorrow.' But you didn't say any of that. You said, 'If you're going to walk with God and do what God says, it's going to take work. You're going to have to be a doer of the Word every day.'"

What he said fascinated me because I thought that was what we were supposed to do when we preach—help people figure out how to live out the gospel in their everyday lives.

One of the reasons I believe God kept me at UPS for so long was so I could learn how hard it is to think God's thoughts while working in a secular world. It's hard work, no doubt about it. Henry Ford famously said, "Thinking is the hardest work there is, which is probably the reason why so few people engage in it."

We won't just accidentally renew our minds; that's not how we become more holy. That's why the apostle Paul tells us that change in Christ is a process of putting off our "old self, which is being corrupted by its deceitful desires" and putting on our "new self, created to be like God in true righteousness and holiness." And how does he say this happens? We learn "to be made new in the attitude of [our] minds" (Ephesians 4:22-24).

It takes intentional effort to engage this process of changing the way we think. D.A. Carson said this about our tendency to drift:

> People do not drift toward Holiness. Apart from grace-driven effort, people do not gravitate toward godliness, prayer, obedience to Scripture, faith, and delight in the Lord. We drift toward compromise and call it tolerance; we drift toward disobedience and call it freedom; we drift toward superstition and call it faith. We cherish the

indiscipline of lost self-control and call it relaxation; we slouch toward prayerlessness and delude ourselves into thinking we have escaped legalism; we slide toward godlessness and convince ourselves we have been liberated.[12]

Does that sound familiar to you? Have you been drifting when it comes to policing your thought life? Have you fallen for believing the lie that your thought life is out of your control?

Another study I found had researchers studying learned helplessness in adults. In this study, researchers assigned two groups the same menial task to finish and placed them both in an atmosphere with a distracting noise. One group of participants had the option of turning off the distracting noise while they worked. The other group was told they could not turn off the noise.

Researchers discovered that even though the first group thought they had the ability to turn off the noise, they often chose not to turn it off. Yet this group performed better, with or without the noise, than the workers who thought they had no control over the noise. Researchers concluded that simply believing that they could do something about their problem helped the first group to succeed while the second group struggled. Simply thinking "I can" instead of "I can't" increased their performance.

So many of us embrace an apathetic, defeatist attitude. We tell ourselves, "Why start? We can't make a difference." How do we know we can't make a difference until we try to make a difference? And how big a difference do we have to make to make it worthwhile? What if changing the way we think makes a difference in one person's life? Is that not a difference?

But we give up too soon. We stop believing, stop thinking, and stop trying to change. If we think we can never take our thoughts captive and think new, God-honoring thoughts, then we'll never even try. But if we believe that we can do all things through Christ who strengthens us, we start to try. Before long we're thinking the opposite thoughts: I can't stop following Christ. I can't stop renewing my mind with the Word of God.

Now those are some "I can't" statements that could change your life.

The Cleansing Word

If we're going to align our thoughts with God's—no easy task—we have to understand that God thinks differently than we do. The Bible says that His ways are higher than our ways. His thoughts are higher than our thoughts (Isaiah 55:9). It's not that we have no access to them; He's made a point of ensuring we can understand all we need to understand to live a better life. His Word is "able to make you wise for salvation through faith in Christ Jesus" and has all we need to "be thoroughly equipped for every good work" (2 Timothy 3:15,17). But God thinks at a level we could never reach.

Thank God that He wrote down so many of His thoughts in the Bible so people like me could get it. I don't know about you, but I need to read and reread and study His Word to make sense of it all. I don't recall exactly what my class rank was when I graduated from high school; I was just glad to pass. If you tried to look for me among the top students in my graduating class, you'd be looking for a long time. I simply didn't care. So I can relate to everyone who struggles to grasp the notion of thinking like God. Believe me, there is still a huge gap between my thoughts and God's thoughts. But as I have followed along with His Word over time, His thinking has changed my thinking.

I came across a Scripture one day years after I'd been saved. Everyone had been telling me that I needed to feel a certain way to have a good relationship with God. But then I read John 14:15: "If you love me, keep my commands." And it changed my thinking. *Oh, God, I get it. You're telling me I don't have to feel anything. I show You I love You by doing what You ask me to do.* When I talk about thinking new thoughts and thinking like God thinks, I mean discovering what His Word says because that's how we know how He thinks.

Another example: God's a God of faith. He has called me to live my life "by faith from first to last" (Romans 1:17). He tells me that "without faith it is impossible to please God" (Hebrews 11:6). Living by faith means I have to believe in something I cannot see. Now, I would prefer that I didn't have to do that because it's not easy. I've said to Him, *God, why do I have to trust You to answer my prayers? Can't I just pray and it happens?* For whatever reason, God requires faith as part of the process. That's how God thinks. It's not how I think or even what I like on most days. But I have learned to try to see life as God sees life by having my mind renewed by His cleansing Word.

Until we learn to see life from God's perspective, we'll never really know how we are to live. God says I should do good to my enemies and pray for those who mistreat me (Luke 6:28). My flesh says, "I want to fight my enemies!" I have to submit my will to God's and say, *God, You know these people are wretched and awful, but when I'm around them, I'll be kind. Not because I want to be kind, but because You've asked me to be kind.* Now why does God ask me to be kind to my enemies? Because God knows that it is often kindness that leads us to repentance and real life-change (Romans 2:4).

That's the power of His Word to change how we think. Jesus Himself prayed that the Father would cleanse us with His Word (John 17:17). The Bible is "inspired by God and is useful to teach us what is true and to make us realize what is wrong in our lives. It corrects us when we are wrong and teaches us to do what is right" (2 Timothy 3:16 NLT). It's that simple. Want to think new thoughts?

Think God's thoughts by meditating on His Word. Let it soak into your life and see if your thoughts don't change.

Just a Thought:
What do you think about?

What do you think about? The Bible says we are to choose to think on positive things, not negative stuff that drains our energy and saps our strength to obey God. If you are becoming what you think about, what percentage of your time is spent in negative regret and misery instead of positive thoughts and hope about your future? People who get ahead possess a different mindset than those who have a victim attitude and learned helplessness mindset. They choose to work diligently, take responsibility, and learn new things. They realize that in order to do better in life, they must continue to work hard, work smart and stay committed. Just a thought...

Tips for Thinking New Thoughts

- *Take destructive thoughts captive.* Identify, isolate, and replace negative thoughts with God's thoughts and not your own. Your own thinking will only get you into more captivity.

- *Limit or eliminate your exposure to negative influences.* Relationships, music, movies—whatever it is that keeps introducing negative thoughts into your life has to go.

- *Encounter God's Word regularly.* There can be no

substitute for the cleansing power of the Bible. If you do not read it, you have no hope for real, lasting change.

- *Be grateful for what God has given you.* Ingratitude is at the root of so much wrong thinking. By choosing to be thankful, you close the door on it.

- *Set achievable goals.* Don't think you will master every thought immediately. Take it one thought, one minute, one day at a time.

- *Don't believe everything that you think.* Just because you have a thought doesn't mean it is good, pure, noble, or right. Hold it up to the Word of God to see if it should be believed.

How God's Thoughts Transform Your Thoughts

When our thoughts begin to line up with God's thoughts, we begin to think differently. The enemy wants us to believe changing our life is not possible; but I have seen it happen in my own life and in the lives of countless others.

Earlier I mentioned my dear friend Brother Haymes, who was one of two people who hired me at the first church I pastored in Roswell. He was a black man and an elder at the church. He used to tell me stories of his childhood, how when he was ten to twelve years old he would shine white men's shoes to help support his family. While he was shining those shoes, the men would sometimes spit on him and call him horrible names. (Just thinking about it now breaks my heart for that little boy. How could people be so cold-hearted and calloused?)

After he told me that story, I asked, "How are you not bitter about that awful treatment? How is it you don't hate white people?"

His response was amazing. He said, "God has given me a great life and blessed my family. I'm so thankful. He wouldn't want me to hate; it would destroy me. So I choose to love people instead and try to help anyone I can to get to know Him."

What an incredible man! I've respected few people as much as I did that dear brother. He overcame by thinking about people the way God thinks about people. Most of us would agree he had every right to hate, to blame, to remain a victim. Instead, he chose to renew his mind and follow God's Word.

When we are negative in our thoughts about people, it's often because either they have done something wrong to us or we think they have done something wrong to us. We tend to focus on the negative rather than choosing to see the positive. We fill our minds with worst-case scenarios, causing worry, anxiety, and fear. The bad part is that we don't have to try to think negatively or fearfully; it comes to us naturally. It's almost as if we're hardwired for unhappy thoughts. According to psychotherapist Tom Moon, we just may be:

> The reason we're like this [focused on negative thoughts] is easy to understand. The brain isn't an organ for objectively studying reality. It's a tool which evolved to anticipate and overcome dangers, protect us from pain, and solve problems: so dangers, pain, and problems are what capture its attention. Neuropsychologist Rick Hanson (www.rickhanson.net) refers to this as "the brain's negativity bias." The human nervous system, he writes "scans for, reacts to, stores, and recalls negative information about oneself and one's world. The brain is like Velcro for negative experiences and Teflon for positive ones.[13]

Though I don't agree with Moon's evolutionary worldview, I think he may be on to something. According to experts, our fight-or-flight reflex gives us five times as many networks to detect threats than to sense positive rewards.[14] Dr. Raj Raghunathan says, "Even though people claim to hold themselves in high regard, the thoughts that spontaneously occur to them—their 'mental chatter,' so to speak—is mostly (up to 70%) negative, a phenomenon that could be referred to as negativity dominance."[15] Is it any wonder that with this biological predisposition to negative thinking, we tend to dwell on negative thoughts?

But in spite of this natural tendency, God calls us to think new thoughts, thoughts that equip us to see the world from God's perspective. The apostle Paul makes it easy by telling us exactly what we *should* think about:

> Finally, brothers and sisters, whatever is true, whatever is noble, whatever is right, whatever is pure, whatever is lovely, whatever is admirable—if anything is excellent or praiseworthy—think about such things. Whatever you have learned or received or heard from me, or seen in me—put it into practice. And the God of peace will be with you (Philippians 4:8-9).

Knowing our tendency to gravitate toward the negative, God tells us there are seven categories of thoughts we should be thinking about daily. When we intentionally and consistently think on these things, we form new habits of thought.

Nineteenth-century philosopher Henry David Thoreau rightly said, "As a single footstep will not make a path on the earth, so a single thought will not make a pathway in the mind. To make a deep physical path, we walk again and again. To make a deep mental path, we must think over and over the kind of thoughts we wish to dominate our lives."[16]

It doesn't happen overnight; it takes time.

The Bible says faith comes from hearing the Word of God (Romans 10:17). If we want to choose new thoughts, thoughts of hope and healing for a better life in Christ, we can't be like those babies in that study who learned to accept their present circumstances. We must intentionally renovate our minds by God's Word. It is living, powerful, and effective (Hebrews 4:12).

If we grow our devotional life, we avoid an emotional life. By consistently exposing ourselves to God's thoughts that He's revealed in the Bible, we become healthier and better equipped to overcome whatever problems we may face.

WHAT YOU CAN DO NOW

- Do you struggle with thoughts you know are not pleasing to God? What do you do when they pop into your head? The Bible tells us that the solution is to flee, to run away from sinful thinking. If you can, leave the place that is triggering those thoughts. If you can't run away physically, list specific, God-honoring thoughts you can "run" to instead when ungodly thoughts come to mind.

- The only way you will ever replace destructive thoughts with God's thoughts is by regularly exposing yourself to His Word. What are you doing to make a habit of reading and studying the Word of God? If it is not already part of your daily routine, choose a time of day that works well for you to get alone with God and His Word.

- Do you find yourself caught in negative thought patterns? How might you replace those negative thoughts with positive thoughts as God calls us to do? Take a moment now to review the categories God gives us and list ways you can focus your thoughts on these things: "whatever is true, whatever is noble, whatever is right, whatever is pure, whatever is lovely, whatever is admirable—if anything is excellent or praiseworthy—think about such things" (Philippians 4:8).

- Don't compare yourself to anyone else. Your growth in Christ is your journey. The Bible warns us not to compare ourselves to one another. Besides, it's a waste of time because you have no way of knowing what another person truly thinks. Be the best you that God created you to be.

9

PLAY THE HAND
YOU'VE BEEN DEALT

I was a mess of discontentedness growing up. Nothing seemed to meet my expectations even though I couldn't even tell you what those expectations were.

I had it pretty good as child— we never lacked food, shelter, or clothing—but I still felt left out. Even after I got saved, I couldn't see my blessings because this attitude got in the way. Now I had someone new to blame: the problems in my life became God's fault. Few could see my lack of confidence on the outside, but every day I was whining on the inside.

Then someone told me something that changed my life, "You have to play the hand you've been dealt." I couldn't get that comment out of my mind; soon it began to change my entire attitude. Here I was wishing I could play life with cards I didn't have. But I can play only the cards I've been dealt. I can't play someone else's hand no matter how much I may want to.

If you've ever played poker, or seen it played in movies or on television, you know that everyone is dealt cards at the outset. The players then work with the cards they have to try to form a winning hand. As the game progresses, a player has three options: he can play, hold, or fold. If he's dealt a bad hand, he can always fold, just walk away with little harm done and play again another time.

But life doesn't work that way, does it? If we fold the hand we're dealt in life, we have no hope, no way to change, and no end in sight. Once we get real about our problems, choose a new direction in Christ, and start thinking new thoughts guided by God's Word, it's time to get busy playing the hand we've been dealt. Folding is not an option, no matter the challenges we face. As athletes often say, pain is temporary, but quitting is forever.

We get into trouble when we ignore the present and look either back into our past or daydream about the future. We all know people who seem to be stuck in the "glory days" of high school. If all we do is long for the past and whine about how we wish we could go back, we're bound to run into obstacles we otherwise might have avoided. On the other hand, when we fantasize about the future but don't take action now, we miss out on God's best for us as well.

To use a baseball metaphor, I love how Dan Buell puts it: "God may call you to something else someday, but you can only hit the pitch being thrown to you at the moment." A lot of us spend our time thinking, *Boy, in the ninth inning, the bases are going to be loaded, I'm going to hit a home run and be a hero!* Meanwhile, here we are in the third inning, asleep as pitch after pitch goes by. By the time the ninth inning comes around, we won't even be in the game. We'll be riding the bench and accusing our heavenly Coach of being unfair.

A Way of Life

Overcomers may hurt. They may cry. They may not have all the answers. But at the end of the day, they cry, "Game on!" Victims fold and blame.

There's a little boy at Legacy Church named Leo who cannot speak a word, and yet he demonstrates to me the simple power of playing the hand we've been dealt. When his mother was six months pregnant with him, Leo was diagnosed with Klinefelter syndrome and agenesis of the corpus callosum. His mother described the moment when her doctor offered abortion as an option. For Leo's mother, who believed God had a purpose for the little boy still in her womb, abortion was not an option. She told her doctor, "My baby is going to live a great life, and he's going to be happy in this life, and God put him in my life for a reason." She refused to fold.

Since he was born, Leo has been diagnosed with many disorders, including one that causes seizures. Leo's struggles mean he will likely never speak, but he inspires the people he meets with his contentment and a smile that his mother says speaks his love for her every day. Leo's mother speaks with certainty when she says, "Leo's proven that he has a purpose here in this world." Even with all the challenges Leo faces, he and his mother continue to play the hands they've been dealt—and God continues to bless through their obedience.

If it's possible for Leo to live out God's plan for his life, it's possible for me, and it's possible for you. When you develop a lifestyle of playing the hand you're dealt, you don't become bitter or resentful or malicious because what you have is not what you want. You believe God can turn for good what Satan meant for evil.

You may recall the story of Joseph from the book of Genesis in the Bible. His brothers hated him and sold him into slavery; he was falsely accused and imprisoned. And yet he continued to play the hand he'd been given, always trusting God while stepping forward wherever he could. As a result, he became the second most powerful person in all of Egypt and saved millions of people from starvation.

But imagine if he had folded. No one would have blamed him after being dealt a hand like that. Yet here is Joseph's perspective when he finally confronted—and forgave—his brothers: "You intended to harm me, but God intended it for good to accomplish what is now being done, the saving of many lives" (Genesis 50:20). He played the hand he'd been dealt and experienced the blessing of God.

We forget that God knows the cards we've been dealt; we didn't get them by chance. He has a plan for us if we are willing to stay in and refuse to fold.

Cynthia's Story

My own wife's story illustrates the power of this truth. Cynthia has had to overcome stuff in her life that would have crushed most people. But she didn't quit. She kept playing the hand she'd been dealt. Once Christ did a work within her, she began trusting God and—well, I'll let her tell you her story in her own words:

> My childhood memories are so vivid. People say kids can't remember stuff, but I remember it all. I had five dads growing up as my mom endured a chain of abusive relationships that started with my mom's second husband.
>
> One time when I was three years old, my mom made a cake for my stepdad's birthday. He'd been drinking before he came home. For no apparent reason, he got angry, picked up the cake, and threw it at my mom. He missed. I can still see it so vividly sliding down the wall. Then he picked up a butcher knife and went after her. My sister and I had been watching from the hall, but when we saw him cut off part of her finger, something snapped inside me. I ran over and bit him on the leg. I clamped down and put a death grip on his calf. My mother told me later that she thought for certain my stepdad was going to stab me.

She pleaded with him to put the knife down. When she finally got me to let go, he staggered into the back bedroom and passed out. My mother, as many victims of domestic abuse will do, went in and bandaged my stepdad's leg. He'd just come after her with a knife, but she still took care of him. Stuff like this would happen, and then my stepdad would be fine for a couple weeks before getting drunk again.

The last incident I remember with him happened when I was four. We were checking out of a hotel, and my stepdad made my mom go pay the bill. When she went inside, he just took off with my sister and me in the car. My sister, who was two years older than I, realized what had happened, opened the door, and shoved me out on the highway and jumped out right behind me.

My stepdad stopped the car a few hundred feet down the highway, but another car had already stopped to help us. My stepdad began backing up toward us as my sister told the people who'd stopped, "He just left my mom at that hotel. Don't let us go with him!" And they didn't. They wouldn't leave until he had gone back and picked up my mom.

But one day, while he was at work, mom found the courage to leave. We moved away and she divorced him. But then she married three more times.

By the time I reached high school, I just wanted to get out of the madness. At seventeen, I had a steady boyfriend who I married right out of high school. My intent was to be a virgin when I got married, which I was, and to stay married forever. I determined not to follow my mother's example.

Everything was going fine until, about eight months into our marriage, he started getting violent. I had always told myself I would never let a man hit me. Well, he hit me. Then he became possessive. He wouldn't let me go shopping with my girlfriends. I had to call him when I got to work and call when I got home. I had to spend the night with my mother, because he worked at night. I wasn't even allowed to stay home by myself. It was crazy.

The first couple of times he hit me, I forgave him and made up lies to explain my bruises to people. The third or fourth time it happened, I told him, "If you ever hit me again, I will divorce you. You need to get help." He said he would.

He did fine for the next few months. Then one day in our apartment, he came after me for no reason, just like my stepdad had done with my mom. I was running from him, jumping over the bed, ducking things he was throwing. Somehow I managed to lock myself in the bathroom.

At that moment, somebody rang our doorbell. Immediately I thought, *This could save me.* My husband warned me through the door, "You'd better be quiet." But I just started praying, *Oh, please, please, God, let me get to that front door somehow.* I didn't even know God at the time, but I knew only He could help me. I knew I had to get to the front door first.

The doorbell rang again. Then someone knocked. I unlocked the bathroom door and turned the handle as quietly as I could. My husband had moved toward the front door. I just kept thinking, *I can't live like this. I can't do this. I can't end up like my mom.* So I went for it. I darted by him, unlocked the front door, and swung it open before he even knew what happened. And there was one of his best friends! He was a big guy, probably six foot six. He could tell I was scared and asked me, "Are you OK?" I said, "No! He's going to kill me!"

I'll never forget what happened next. That big guy picked up my husband and threw *him* down the stairs. I was saved. But you know what I did then? I went down those stairs to see how he was, just like my mom had done with my stepdad.

Later, I told him it was over. I refused to live in fear. I got a divorce, all the time beating myself up for that, because I thought, *I am doing the same thing my mother did.* I decided I was never getting married or dating again.

Well, four years later, I met another guy. We got engaged, but I refused to sleep with him before we were married. It was another line I had drawn for myself. But one night, things happened and we crossed that line. The next day I cried so hard, thinking I was no better than my mom. I beat myself up about it. After I found out I was pregnant, I called off the wedding. I had begun seeing signs that I was heading toward another abusive relationship, and so I changed direction. I decided I'd rather raise the baby by myself. I had a girl and her dad walked out of her life. And I raised her on my own until I met Steve.

That's when my life began to turn. I had refused to quit through all I had experienced, but it was through Steve that I encountered God. But even through all the crazy hard times, even before I was saved, I never walked around thinking I was a victim or that I had been beaten. I beat *myself* up for being divorced and having a baby without being married, but I was determined to keep playing the hand I'd been dealt, to not let my circumstances ruin me.

There's nothing I can do about the past. I can't change it or make up for it or fix it. Life is way too short to stay in the past with the junk and sadness and hurts. That's my philosophy. I let the past go, and in the end, God freed me from it all.

How to Identify Self-Sabotaging Behaviors

If you're like most people, you'd say you have a busy life. But you can be busy with a lot of things and still be engaged in behaviors that are self-sabotaging. Take an objective look to see if what's keeping you busy is helping or hurting. Ask yourself these two clarifying questions:

1. Do you fear success?

2. Do you fear failure?

People who fear either of these often sabotage their future without realizing why. They start to do well, then something always happens. They start moving up the ladder, being noticed, or receiving promotions. Then, like clockwork, they start fixating on something they don't like or feel is unfair. Or something goes wrong in their personal life and they start making poor decisions and blaming everyone but themselves. Their reaction to adversity is always the same destructive beliefs that destroy their opportunities.

This is just one way we self-sabotage instead of playing the hand we've been dealt. Do you always seem to be starting over? Are you constantly telling yourself, *This time will be different*? If you haven't changed how you think, you will revert to what is the most comfortable for you when pressure arrives. The most prevalent thought in our mind will come out of us naturally. We can handle only one belief system at a time. This is another reason why we must transform our thinking. Change your thinking and you will eliminate the self-sabotaging behaviors.

What Happens When We Act

As my wife's story demonstrates, we find a better life when we keep moving forward. I'm not saying finding me is what saved her, but finding God transformed her life. Her actions revealed her refusal to settle for less than something more.

So it is with all of us. When we commit to acting with the knowledge and ability we have at the moment, opportunities that we never realized before begin to present themselves. That's how God's universe works. Someone described the power of that commitment in this way:

> The moment one definitely commits oneself, then Providence [God] moves too. All sorts of things occur to help one that would never otherwise have occurred. A whole stream of events issue from the decision, raising in one's favor all manner of unforeseen incidents and meetings and material assistance, which no man could have dreamed would come his way.[17]

I know that has certainly been true for me. I once never dared to dream I could have as good a life as I have now. I'm not referring to physical blessings necessarily, but to the relationships, fulfillment, joy, and real peace that God has given me. If I had simply checked out back when I was a UPS driver, I do not believe I would be here now. But I have learned what happens when we have the courage to act with what has been given to us instead of whining about what we think we want but don't have.

Our actions make change real to us. Until we do something, our new direction is just fantasy. Action turns fairy tales into biographies. They move our belief from imagination to reality. And sometimes we are the ones who most need to see us in motion. By taking action where we can today, we boost our own confidence to tackle the challenges of tomorrow.

Our actions create momentum. Each step we take empowers us to take one more. John C. Maxwell calls this the power of The Big Mo. The victim mentality says to wait until God makes all as it should be before taking action; but I agree with a well-known Christian saying: "Pray like it depends on God; act as if it depends on you." As we move, we build confidence in God and in our own ability that He has given to us.

Our actions send a signal to others that we have changed. When we begin to take action based on our new direction, other people will see it. When I was working at UPS, I put an envelope package in a mail slot, thinking the mailman had come and gone already. UPS policy is that we could never, ever put anything in a mailbox. You could lose your job for it. But it was a steaming summer afternoon in Broken Arrow, Oklahoma, and I was tired. So I put it in there.

A few days later, my supervisor called me in and asked if I had delivered a package to that address. When the mailman had delivered the mail, he'd seen the package and returned it to the sender. I knew full well the ramifications of what I had done. Everything in me was screaming, "Lie!" All I had to do was say, "I don't remember," and it would have been over with.

But I knew it wouldn't be pleasing to God. Instead, I told my supervisor what had happened. He gave me a shocked look I will never forget.

"You know I could fire you now," he said.

"Yes."

"But because you were honest about it, I'll let it go. But don't you ever do it again."

I thanked him profusely and never made that mistake again.

Our actions raise our awareness of options. Only when we begin to move can we see things from a fresh perspective. We can't see what is in our blind spots if we always stay in the same place. A healthy perspective is one that keeps moving forward at all times. If we fold, we have no more options.

Strategies for Making Progress

If you see the need to take responsibility for your life and take action, but you feel trapped by destructive patterns of behavior, here are a few practical suggestions for replacing negative behaviors with positive ones.

Cut off all access. The biblical command regarding anything that derails us is to avoid it, don't go near it, run from it, and flee (Proverbs 4:15). That's what Joseph did literally when Potiphar's wife was determined to get him in bed with her. He ran. It's what I did when tempted so many years ago by the pretty girl outside the bank.

The writer of Hebrews says to "lay aside every encumbrance and the sin which so easily entangles us," so we can "run with endurance the race that is set before us" (Hebrews 12:1 NASB). When we fail to aggressively cut off access to negative behavior, we set ourselves up for failure. The fight simply saps our strength and wears us down over time. One way we self-sabotage the change process is by intentionally permitting access, giving ourselves an excuse to slip back into destructive behaviors.

Create consequences. Like a small child, we may not get the message that the stove is hot until we feel the pain. We can set up painful consequences that alert us when we start to engage in negative behavior. It may be accountability partners who check in on us. If you know you will sometimes try to hide the truth even from them, set up an objective system to alert them when you step in the wrong direction. We can create environments that do not let us get away with slipping back into negative behaviors. We should also set up ways to enjoy the benefits of staying on course. For example, an addict can reward himself in some way for each day, week, or month he stays clean. Another person could reward herself each time she doesn't give in to negative self-talk.

Identify the triggers. The Bible says that each of us sins when we are led away by our own sinful desires (James 1:14). So what are the desires that seem to pull you back into negative behavior patterns? What triggers them? By identifying those triggers, you can make plans to avoid situations that trigger unhealthy responses.

Replace the triggers. Once you identify the triggers, you need to replace them with healthy responses. Instead of a stressful situation at work leading you to head to the bar for a few drinks, replace that potentially destructive behavior with a new pattern, perhaps coffee with your accountability partner or a season of prayer with your spouse, a walk in nature, or even working out at the gym. By replacing your trigger, you choose your response to the circumstances.

Set up guardrails. Job tells us (Job 31:1) that he has set up protective blinders to keep his eyes from wandering where they should not go—not because of a particular crisis but as a general life practice. We too can set up guardrails as a general life practice to keep us on course. Wherever we might slip, we should put up barriers so it is difficult to stumble. The moment we think we've got things under control, we are at risk of falling face-first back into our negative behaviors.

Keep your "why" in focus. The core of our motivation must be love for God and appreciation for His grace in our lives. Never forget where you came from and what He's done for you. Beyond that, we all have additional motivation for change. Yours may be different from everyone else's. Maybe it's getting healthy, achieving a dream of a college degree, making a goal to open your own business, or leaving a legacy for your family. What's your motivation?

Once you've clarified it, keep it front and center. Make it your first thought each morning. Post it where you can read it. Wear a bracelet that symbolizes your goal. Choose a song that reminds you. There's no shortage of creative ways to keep it in focus. Just do it.

Opportunities come to those who focus on doing what they can with what they've been given. Right here. Right now. The truth is that if we keep moving and keep playing the hand we've been dealt, eventually we'll get better cards.

I am not saying it will be easy—not at all. Sometimes unexpected stuff just knocks the wind out of you. When that would happen to me back in my days of high school football, the coaches would roll me onto my back and pull up on my belt. Maybe it forced me to breathe again. Maybe it just made them feel useful. I don't know. But it made me think they had seen this before and everything was going to be OK. That's what we all need to realize: no matter the problems that blindside us, we will breathe again because God is with us. And He's been there, done that.

No matter what you face right now, God is bigger. Jesus knows the hand you've been dealt, and still He says, "all things are possible with God" (Mark 10:27). But only if we're committed to playing the hand we've been dealt.

WHAT YOU CAN DO NOW

- Think about a problem in your life. What does the Bible say should be your goal in dealing with it? Identify a plan to overcome it: How do I get there? What are the roadblocks, what are the stumbling blocks, what keeps me from arriving? If this is the promise of God, what keeps me from receiving it? Finally, am I self-sabotaging?

- Set goals—you can't get there if you don't know where "there" is. Where do you want to go? What dreams and aspirations has God given you? If you don't know where to go, find someone who can give some vision for your life, someone who can say, "This is where you could be." Often we don't see our own potential or where we would be a good fit in serving the kingdom of God, but someone else often will have a number of ideas about where we'd be the perfect fit.

- Understand your goal and realize what it takes to reach that goal. If it's a small goal, you might get there in a week, a month, a year. If it's a bigger goal, break it down into smaller goals or milestones so you don't get discouraged. Like we said before, taking action leads to success and success leads to momentum to keep going. For big goals, little successes along the way are so important.

- God asked Moses, "What is that in your hand?" (Exodus 4:2). Then He used that stick to help deliver the Israelites out of Egyptian slavery. God will give you more based on what you do with what you have. What are you doing with what God has given you? Are you being faithful with what you have, because those who are faithful with what they have will be given more to steward.

10

CONNECT WITH A CARING COMMUNITY

Michelangelo would probably be dead now if he had not connected to a caring church community. I'm not talking about the guy who painted the Sistine Chapel hundreds of years ago. I'm talking about a young man who found new life in Christ here at Legacy Church.

As he tells his story, Michelangelo didn't know he needed Christ until he found himself in jail facing a twenty-five-year sentence for a domestic dispute. Suddenly he saw where his lifestyle of partying, irresponsibility, drugs, and homosexuality was leading him. He thought his life was over. With nothing left to lose, he went to a prayer gathering at the prison and was overwhelmed with a warmth and peace he'd never felt before. His fear began to turn to joy, and he knew he needed more.

When the state unexpectedly dropped his charges, Michelangelo was a free man. But free to do what? He didn't want to return to the lifestyle he had known before. He weighed only ninety pounds at the time, the black marks on his face revealing that he was HIV-positive. In fact, the disease had advanced so far that most people are dead by the time they reach this stage. He knew he'd fall right back into his old lifestyle unless he found a good church. But he wondered if any Christians would accept him as he was.

Michelangelo took the risk and checked out Legacy Church. On the very first Sunday, he responded to an altar call and totally surrendered his life to Christ. At Legacy, he found a family that accepted him even as messy as he was. With the help of his new church family, he began to grow spiritually and strengthen physically. Three years later, he sat down with his bewildered doctor who gave him a bewildered report. "You're undetectable," she said. "We can't find the virus in your body." She couldn't use the word *healed*, but he says that he knows in his heart he is—and he has the paperwork to show it. Michelangelo says, "The world tells me that's impossible, but I have a God who tells me through Him all things are possible."

In his own words, Michelangelo has gone from "a man who was gay, late-stage HIV, addicted to drugs, angry, and just a complete mess—to a man who's still a little messy, still in desperate need of Christ all the time, but healed, transformed, renewed, grateful, and thankful." His story is a testimony both to the power of God and the power of connecting with God's people. "If it wasn't for the people here at Legacy who loved me, helped me, and endured with me," he says, "I would not be alive today."

Created for Community

It's not just the desperate among us who need a caring community to overcome problems. If we're honest about it, we're all desperate for connection with others. And that shouldn't surprise us because God created us for community. At creation he said, "It is not good for the man to be alone" (Genesis 2:18). So he created woman and launched the first human relationship, the first family. But it was not the first community, for God Himself is a community. In the mystery of the Trinity, the Father, Son, and Holy Spirit have an ongoing, eternal relationship. Community is at the very core of who God is. It should not surprise us then that Adam and Eve were made for relationship with God and with each other.

But that first family had troubles, just as all of our families do today. Once sin entered the world, our basic need to connect with others became that much more critical, even as that first family fell into chaos, betrayal, and even murder. Thankfully, God made another family, a broader community of support built on an unshakeable foundation—Jesus Christ. Through authentic connection with our new brothers and sisters in Christ, we find support and strength to do all things through Christ. That's not to say that the people you'll meet in God's family are perfect or that we always agree. But we will always be there for each other. If you want to live a better life, you have to surround yourself with people who share your faith and who love you no matter how you fail.

Unfortunately, too many people in the church lack mercy when it comes to failure, both in other people and in themselves. The church should be a place where we accept each other as is and help each other faithfully follow God's direction to live a better life—together. People will fall. They will disappoint. It's a fact of life. But it's a thousand times more challenging to get back up when you are alone.

God's people shouldn't write people off because God doesn't write people off. Remember that the God of the Bible is the God of another chance, no matter how many times we may fall. The Bible says that He is quick to show mercy, as if He is always ready, poised to show undeserved favor at any time (Psalm 103:8). But the church is not God. We're not perfect, so we don't always get it right.

Brent discovered that the church can disappoint. He was one of those teenagers who partied every chance he got. When he was twenty, he found out he'd gotten a girl pregnant. His family responded by telling Brent that he'd messed up his life forever and encouraging an abortion. People at his church turned their back on him. They wouldn't let him be involved anymore because he had a son without being married. Right when he needed his support system the most, it caved in around him.

So Brent did what a lot of people do when the church fails. He got mad. He left the church and went his own way. It was some time later that a friend invited him to join a motorcycle group here at Legacy Church. Yes, you read that right; we have a motorcycle group here called the Legacy Riders. Brent rode with them for a while but always blew off their invitations to come to a church service. Finally, he agreed to come to just one.

When we extended a call to come forward and make things right with God, Brent found himself up front wondering, *What kind of legacy am I leaving for my son?* He knew it was not a good one. And he wanted that to change. He adopted the Legacy Riders' motto as his own: "Leaving a legacy as we ride." His new church family here at Legacy helped him to stop smoking and drinking and to become a better person by following God's Word.

The defining moment for Brent came a couple years later when his brother, a marine, was injured in duty. The crisis tested Brent and his family as his extended family looked to him for spiritual leadership and words of comfort and prayer. Because of what he'd learned at Legacy, he was able to step up and be there. They started seeing miracles as Brent's brother was stabilized and brought back to the States. He recovered and is whole and healthy today. Brent knows now that the troubles he went through before taught him the value of a caring, Christ-centered community. Without God and God's people, he wouldn't have known how to cope with trials and wouldn't have been able to see his family through their most challenging time.

A caring church community should love you through anything, even as it calls you to get back up and keep walking when you make a mistake. That's what the God of another chance does for us and what we must do for one another.

You Are Not Alone

So many times I've called or texted people out of the blue saying, "Hey, I'm thinking about you. I'm praying." And they'll text a whole letter back saying, "Oh, you have no idea. I'm dealing with this and this. It was just good to know someone was thinking about me." I believe we are weakest when we're alone. We can't do anything without the power of God, and more often than not, God works through the people around us, especially fellow believers.

The writer of Hebrews tells us we should not be "forsaking or neglecting to assemble together [as believers], as is the habit of some people, but admonishing (warning, urging, and encouraging) one another" (Hebrews 10:25 AMP). God has commanded us in His Word to gather together with other believers and talk about how to live out the truths of the Bible. In other words, it's not optional.

If that is true, why is this step the most neglected on the pathway to a better life? Why do we think we don't need each other? Why do we insist on going it alone? The answer is that we have an enemy who knows how vital that support is to our growth. Satan will do everything he can to keep us from living a better life. Aided by our own sinful stubborn streaks, he can be very effective at isolating struggling Christians. Unfortunately, many people today deny that the devil even exists. They say he's nothing more than an old-fashioned character designed to scare children into obeying. But the Bible is clear: Satan is real. He goes by many names, but Jesus said he has one focus: to steal, kill, and destroy (John 10:10).

A deceiver by nature, the devil works to isolate us from each other so we miss out on the encouragement and accountability that will make us grow. He wants us to think we are alone, that the problems we face are unlike those anyone else has ever faced. I can't count how many times people are surprised when I tell them, "You are not the only one who has gone through this." I tell them story after story of others who've gone through the same exact thing and come out on the other side. I read them 1 Corinthians 10:13, which basically says, "Whatever you are going through, rest assured there are others who have gone through the same stuff."

The enemy uses lies to isolate us from the Word of God, the church, and other Christians. When we stay rooted and planted in the church, we find safety. If the enemy can get us away from the rest of the flock and into the wilderness, he will destroy us. And he knows it.

What Happens When You Connect

When you genuinely connect with a caring church community, you will see real life-change just as Brent did. Getting involved in a church family takes effort, but the benefits far outweigh the challenges. And I say that as a pastor who sees both the benefits and the challenges firsthand each and every day. Here are just a few opportunities you give yourself when you connect with a caring church community.

Surround yourself with positive peer pressure. Peer pressure can work both positively and negatively. We all know how the negative pressure works, but we can put peer pressure to work in a positive way when we surround ourselves with other people committed to living a better life in Christ. They push us on to do what we know we need to do, especially when we get tired or lose motivation.

In his book *The 21 Irrefutable Laws of Leadership*, John Maxwell describes what he calls the Law of the Inner Circle. In short, it says that your potential is determined by those closest to you. When we minister to people through our prison ministry, we tell them as they leave prison that they have to cut off a lot of their old friendships, because if they go back to their old friends and hangouts, they'll just end up back in the same mess. Not everyone likes hearing it, but I've had guys tell me a year later, "I did exactly what you said. And you know what? I have a good job. I'm getting married. My life is different."

Let others help carry your burdens. We all go through tough stuff at times. Circumstances arise that we can't handle on our own. Your church family is there to help you, whether by giving counsel or encouragement or by offering practical helps like finding a job, bringing meals, or giving a ride to the doctor when your car breaks down. In Galatians 6:2, the apostle Paul tells Christians to "carry each other's burdens, and in this way you will fulfill the law of Christ." And that instruction applies to you as well.

Offer a helping hand to others. It's not just about you anymore when you plug into a caring community—and that's a good thing. We need to serve others. Being connected and serving others in a church environment keeps you from becoming consumed with yourself, your needs, and your desires. Think of it as an antidote to pride, selfishness, and a host of other sins that so easily throw us off course.

Equip yourself to resist temptation. One of the chief benefits to regularly attending a Bible-believing church is that you expose yourself to truth as it is preached, taught, and shared in small groups. And truth is something we don't get much of in our culture. At Legacy Church, we offer a course titled "The Cleansing Word" because we believe that our hearts are cleaned when we regularly expose them to God's Word. His Word increases our ability to resist temptation and decreases our tendency to stumble into sin.

Raise your protection level. When others are watching out for you, you increase your defense against Satan's attacks. Solomon tells us that "a cord of three strands is not quickly broken" (Ecclesiastes 4:12). When you give permission to others to speak the truth in love to you, it is more difficult to drift into destructive victim thinking. You need people who love you and who are willing to say what needs to be said to you—even if it hurts.

Position yourself for another chance. Have you messed up in life? Welcome to the club. The church is not made up of perfect people—we are all sinners saved by God's grace. We all need forgiveness. Like Michelangelo, you can find a new start with new company, one that will inspire and empower you and ensure you don't slip back into your old ways.

Prepare yourself for the inevitable crisis. Jesus said, "In this world you will have trouble. But take heart! I have overcome the world" (John 16:33). We should expect adversity. Hard times will come, according to Christ. But you can prepare for those hard times, even if you can't yet identify them in detail, by connecting with a caring church community. When you do, you prepare for the crises that inevitably come to us all. You can arm yourself ahead of time with knowledge of the Scriptures and the truth about God while building a support system both for you and for others.

Just a Thought:
How Firm Is Your Foundation?

The Bible teaches that storms will come to all our lives. No matter how well you live, no matter how much you believe and trust in God, storms will come. The question is will you be ready?

Only God and His Word will give you the solid foundation you can build your life on. We must get the Word deep in us, into our core beliefs, so that acting on it becomes more and more our natural response. Being a part of a local church will help you build that solid foundation. A Bible-believing church will help you learn what God's Word teaches and increase your determination to obey it. The Bible itself says that just hearing or knowing the truth—agreeing with the truth—isn't enough. A good church will help you become a doer of the Word and not just a hearer (James 1:22), so you can have a firm foundation when life's storms arrive.

So how firm is your foundation? Just a thought....

How to Find a Healthy Church Community

Are you presently connected to a church community? Is it healthy? Are you looking for a church where you can plug in, learn, and grow? You may have noticed there are a lot of churches out there and not all of them are healthy. Not all of them line up with God's Word. Here are some questions to ask when trying to choose a church that will help you on your pathway to a better life.

Is the church growing? Every healthy thing grows. I've heard all kinds of excuses from pastors over the years about why their churches are not growing. Most churches in America today grow only when people come from another church down the street. Real growth should result from lives being transformed, not seating assignments being shuffled.

How is the church growing? Church growth is not just about numbers. It matters *how* the church is growing. A child can get bigger eating junk food, but we don't call that healthy growth. Many leaders today use fads and slick marketing tricks to grow the church. But unless God builds the house, the people labor in vain (Psalm 127:1). Are people getting saved at the church? Are they coming, staying, committing, and serving—or are the numbers just from a large volume of visitors who only attend? There is no such thing as casual Christianity.

Do they teach the Word of God accurately, or do they water it down? God and His Word are one; they can't be separated. We don't get to pick and choose parts of the Bible to leave out in fear of offending the hearer. Jesus taught the truth without apology, and people either received it or they didn't. He wasn't afraid of people walking away. (Read John 6:53-70 for an example.) The Bible warns us against preachers who only say what people want to hear (2 Timothy 4:3; see also 2 Timothy 3:1-5). Too many pastors act like CEOs trying to attract customers and not like preachers of the gospel trying to save souls from hell. God says, "Those who honor me I will honor, but those who despise me will be disdained" (1 Samuel 2:30). Watered-down Christianity won't help you grow.

Do they give people an opportunity to receive Christ as Savior and Lord? At Legacy Church, we still do something not many churches do anymore, and certainly not most churches this large. We offer an altar call at the end of each service. We want to give people the chance to come down front and get things right with God while the Holy Spirit is convicting their hearts. Not every church has to do it this way, but too many churches today teach that we can negotiate with God or work our way to salvation. The only way to come to God is on His terms, not ours. We must come humbly, surrendering our whole life to Christ and choosing to believe the whole Word of God.

Does the church believe in the power of God to heal and deliver you from bondage? When church leaders talk about dealing with problems, listen to how they describe the power of God or the work of the Holy Spirit to change and transform lives. If you don't hear much about it, chances are good that they don't really believe it. So many church leaders don't believe that the Holy Spirit is present and active today. Pay attention to whether they offer resources that point you to God and His power (biblical counsel, Bible studies, classes) or to man's wisdom.

Is the church engaging the culture around it? Jesus has called us to go into the entire world and preach the gospel, not to limit God's truth to the confines of the church building. That means that a healthy church is focused on taking the good news of Christ to the surrounding community and throughout the world.

But it also means that it stands up to the surrounding culture when it is wrong. Does the church confront the immoral attitudes of the day or go along with what the world says? The church is the moral compass of this world. Without the church, society would be even worse than it is, if you can imagine that! A church that isn't a light in the culture is not healthy. It will not help you or anyone else grow.

The Power of Service

Many years ago, my wife and I were trying to find a church after moving to Tulsa, Oklahoma. We visited one called Church on the Move. Before we heard any music or heard the pastor preach, my wife said, "This is the church we should choose." Why? We saw people serving at that church.

When we first walked up to the church, we weren't sure where to go. We had kids whose ages ranged from early teens to two years old, so they all had different classrooms. A lady saw us near the door and came up to talk to us. She was holding a baby, she seemed about eight months pregnant, and she had a cast on her leg. She asked if we were new and the ages of our children. They would be going to two separate buildings for their classes. She said, "Let me show you." We said, "No, just point us in the right direction." But she absolutely insisted.

Just picture it: this very pregnant woman, with a broken leg no less, carrying another baby on her hip while hobbling around with a whole family of visitors to show them where to go. I don't know how she did it, but she got us everywhere we needed to go. It said something about the church culture that she would joyfully put the needs of others ahead of her own comfort.

We saw another servant in action when we dropped off our youngest child. She didn't like to leave us; whenever we took her to the nursery, she would scream and cry and make a huge fuss. My wife and I always felt awful about being "that family" whose child makes such a scene. But the nursery worker took her, still screaming and crying, and told us, "I'll hold her until she calms down."

Wow! What a moment of clarity for us. Now, twenty-five years later, Pastor Willie George from Church on the Move is still my pastor. He has been one of the most significant voices in shaping my ministry. And it was all because a few people loved God and cared about people enough to serve.

Here's the deal. Whether you've been saved for a day or for years, you need to be involved in a church. Service helps others. But it also helps you as you get involved. And I don't mean just the showing-up-on-Sundays type of involved. I mean the kind of service where if you don't show up, someone notices. They'll call you up if you don't show and see how you're doing. They'll notice when you're hurting because they'll see you all the time. You'll have people you can go to when you need advice, a listening ear, or some prayer. You'll find other people who have the same story as you and can help you walk through your struggles.

I've had people call me at Legacy Church upset because they went into the hospital and no one from the church visited. Right away, I ask them, "What ministry are you involved in?" In most cases, they aren't involved at all. So then I ask, "Well, how are we supposed to know about it? Through osmosis? Is a birdie just supposed to drop in and tell us you are in the hospital?" The reason no one knew what was going on with them is that *they didn't know anyone because they were not serving anywhere.* My encouragement to them is always the same: get involved so that if that happens again, we'll all know.

There's a counterintuitive principle here that you've probably seen at work in your own life. The more we give to others, the more we get in return. Have you ever heard someone say, "You can't out give God"? Have you heard someone come back from a missions trip and say, "I went to minister, but I ended up being blessed more than the people I ministered to"?

This is true throughout the Christian walk. We find greater strength for our own walk when we help others in theirs. Serving God together with pure motives and a good attitude creates such a bond between brothers and sisters in Christ. If you're an usher, and you show up on time, serve with a smile, and stick to it, over time you'll create a circle of friends around you who can help you. You tell them about your life, your relationship with God, and your struggles, and you give them permission to challenge you: "Why are you still letting that defeat you? Why are you thinking this way? Why are you still blaming this person? Why do you see yourself like this?" Friends like that help you truly change your thinking and, therefore, your life direction.

We see this all the time at Legacy. When people come to us struggling with some issue, we ask them about their service. Are you serving? Are you consistent and faithful? Do you serve joyfully or do you have a bad attitude about it? Because we know that Christians are most healthy when they are serving and giving to others. It's not just the fact that we need bodies to do all the stuff that needs to get done around the church—it's about giving our people the chance to be obedient and to access all the benefits of serving. As you give and bless someone else, God is going to help you.

I tell my congregation this regularly. Serving is just something believers do. No ifs, ands, or buts. When you trusted Jesus as your Savior, God's Spirit gave you a spiritual gift or gifts for the purpose of helping others in the church community. It might be related to a talent you already have, or it might be something new you've never tried before. Getting involved in service is how you find out what gift God has given you—and once you find it and start using it, you'll find a sense of joy and fulfillment in doing what God equipped you to do!

How Engaged Are You in Service?

It's better to know where you stand with your church community before a crisis comes. Here are some questions to gauge how engaged you are in service:

- Are you serving? Where do you serve? Why do you serve? Seriously, think for a couple minutes about your motives for serving. Why did you pick the ministry you're in? Are you serving for the limelight?

- Where are you gifted? God chooses what talents to give people; we don't get to return or exchange His gifts. Even if it's not the most glamorous job, you'll be most effective, most fulfilled, most obedient, and most pleasing to God when you serve in an area where He's gifted you.

- Are you faithful in your service? Answer this question honestly. If everyone treated the church like you do, would it be thriving and growing or would it have to close its doors for lack of help and resources? You know your own effort and commitment. Judge yourself.

- What changes do you need to make in how you serve? What steps can you take right now to start in a new direction?

Giving that Grows Our Faith

Being part of a healthy local church is essential to your growth in Christ. If you're not connected to the body, you won't succeed. I've never met anyone who is growing and experiencing spiritual success who is *not* part of the local body. In fact, I often use three questions to see where someone is spiritually:

1. How often do you go to church?

2. Do you serve at your church?

3. Do you tithe?

The answers to those three questions tell a lot about a person's faith. Some people erroneously think those three things represent the epitome of Christian living—if they do all three, they've arrived. But I call them the fundamentals of Christianity. If you're not involved in a local church, you're in the wilderness on your own, and the wilderness is not a place where sheep survive alone for long.

It may be that you're still hung up on that last question. Tithing?

Really? Perhaps you think that tithing, giving a tenth of your income to God's church, is something only old-fashioned legalists still believe. I've heard that a lot. And yet the Bible is clear that giving is a critical piece of a Christian's life.

As our culture moves farther away from God and His Word, more people are making excuses or trying to build a logical case as to why parts of God's Word are no longer relevant. Tithing is one of those things we try to get out of.

I recently saw a survey that said only 3 percent of all Christians tithe. Only 3 percent! No wonder we don't experience the blessings of God in our lives. The worst part is that the Bible presents the tithe as just the minimum we should be giving. God calls us to give offerings on top of that to further show our trust and gratefulness to Him.

If you say, "Well, God understands I just can't give right now," that is victim thinking that will stifle your growth. There's never an option *not* to obey God's Word. It's our handbook for a better life, our roadmap for living. God's Word is powerful and effective (Hebrews 4:12). There is absolutely no reason to ever not follow it. None!

That is what the prophet Samuel told King Saul when he became impatient and tried to make his own way to please God:

> "Does the LORD delight in burnt offerings and sacrifices
>   as much as in obeying the Lord?
> To obey is better than sacrifice,
>   and to heed is better than the fat of rams."
>   (1 Samuel 15:22)

The real issue isn't the money; the real issue is our hearts. Will we obey God or not? Will we trust Him or keep trying our own way? This is where you really prove whether you're serious about following God or not.

I believe 80 to 85 percent of the people who go to our churches are not true believers. Most people who call themselves Christians are just attenders; very few Christians actually involve themselves fully in the local church, but they are the ones who prove that their faith is real.

General Sam Houston, famous for leading Texas to independence in the 1800s, was a rough man, coarse and belligerent before he submitted his life to Christ. When Houston was baptized, he offered to pay half the local minister's salary. When someone asked him why, he said, "My pocketbook was baptized too." Houston believed that when he came to Christ, his money came with him. There was no room for excuses.[18]

Excuses are for victims. Faith champions just do what is right, even when it seems scary and uncomfortable. The Word says, "Without faith it is impossible to please God, because anyone who comes to him must believe that he exists and that he rewards those who earnestly seek him" (Hebrews 11:6).

Do we believe in God when it comes to the money He's given us? Tithing and giving to our local church may test our faith in the midst of trying circumstances. But when we obey His Word, we see Him work. He fulfills His promises to us. And our faith grows.

Warning: Don't Expect Perfection from the Church

One last thought: Don't expect to find a perfect church. No church is perfect because it is full of imperfect people—just like you. God is the only one who is perfect—always good, kind, gentle, and longsuffering. Too many people look to other people to be perfect instead of looking to God who is doing the work within us to make us more like Jesus.

People often tell me they left some other church "because someone hurt me" or "nobody spoke to me when I went there." I come back with this question: "Did *you* speak to anyone when you went to that church?" Almost always, the answer is no. I then ask, "I wonder who won't come back to the church or who will give up on God because *you* didn't speak to them?"

Almost without fail, they had never thought about the impact of their behavior on others, only of how they felt. It's a victim mentality that always demands from others what we are unwilling to do ourselves. It thinks only about itself, the fact that someone else hurt *me*. Someone said something that offended *me,* so *I'm* going to quit going to church or quit serving God.

How ridiculous is it to let someone else's mistakes control you! That's like saying to someone, "I can't be your friend anymore because this other person who you don't know hurt me." What do you think that person would say to you? Would they think you were acting reasonably? Why do we think we can somehow take it out on God when human beings are human and make mistakes?

Here's what we should be thinking instead: *I'm not going to allow anyone to cause me not to serve God.* When we have that mindset, real change will begin to take place. Real hope will come alive.

We need to take responsibility for our lives and not allow ourselves to be the victims of what someone in the church does or says to us. Even if it is bad—and trust me, I know that serious hurts and offenses happen even in church life. They just do. But even if a monster hurt you and stole your innocence, the church is not a place you should run away from. It's there to give you critical support that will overwhelm you with encouragement in your darkest moments, if you can trust other people and let them minister to you in your pain.

I am so incredibly grateful to my own church for how they responded when we had a crisis in our family a few years ago. When our youngest daughter was in college, she walked away from God and the church. Then one night she told my wife and me something that just broke our hearts: she was pregnant.

I was so broken. I started thinking about quitting the ministry. If my own daughter walked away, how could I lead other people? For five months, we didn't tell anyone. We didn't know what to do. We didn't know how the church would respond. We were supposed to be leaders in the church, so we didn't see how we could burden someone else with our problems. Eventually we realized we'd have to do something.

I finally told the church elders. And I was brutally honest with them: "Listen, guys, I'll never hurt the church. I'll resign. I'll do whatever you need me to do." But do you know what they did? Those men just sat there and cried with me. They weren't angry or anything. They just cared about me. And they wouldn't let me resign. For five months we'd been broken inside with no one to help us because we were afraid to open up to our own church family.

That season in my life taught me much about forgiveness (another story for another time). But at that moment, God started healing me. It took a long time, but it all started right there when I opened up to a caring church community, and they responded with the authentic love of Christ.

WHAT YOU CAN DO NOW

Go through the questions in this chapter to help you identify a healthy church. Use them to evaluate your own local church. Do you need to find a healthier church? If your church is a healthy church, thank God—and ensure you are actively contributing to keep it that way.

If you are looking for a church to call home, take a moment now to review the questions about a healthy church. Then pray for God's direction before getting into a church this Sunday, if not sooner. One piece of advice: unless you know right away that it's not a good church, give each place you visit a few weeks so you can see what they're really about. Often, you can't get a complete picture from just one visit.

Ask yourself these questions to evaluate your involvement in your local church community:

- When the word is being preached, do you experience conviction in your heart? God's Word is living and powerful. If it isn't affecting you, the problem isn't with His Word.

- Church is a community, but it should not be just a social gathering. God doesn't want only to give you more friends; he wants you to grow more like Him. Do you meditate on what you've learned throughout the week, or do you forget what you heard?

- Is your church filled with people just like you? People tend to want to be around people like themselves, but I believe we should be a church for everybody. Find another Christian in your local church who is different from you and talk about what you have in common in Christ.

- Is there anyone at your church who has permission to challenge you if they think you are wrong?

- Do you know the people you're serving with in your church, or do you "clock in and clock out" when serving?

- Do you tithe generously and with a joyful heart? If not, why not? Are these valid reasons to disobey God?

11

TRUST GOD ENOUGH TO KEEP MOVING FORWARD

When my son Stevie was a boy, he would always get the latest *Madden NFL* video game for Christmas. Every year I watched the same thing happen. He would get super excited about the new game and try to play it right away. But the controls were different than the previous version and the graphics were new and improved, so he had to adjust how he played the game. Almost every time, he'd get frustrated and finally reach a point when he'd say, "I can't figure this out. I just want to quit! This game is stupid!" I always told him, "Stevie, you're going to figure it out and then you're going to love it." I'd make him keep playing, and soon his attitude would change as he mastered the new version. Before long, he would say, "You were right, Dad. I love it now!"

I was the same way when I was his age. If anything got difficult, I just wanted to quit. I don't think Stevie and I are the only ones who struggle with this. It seems that more than ever in our society, we want instant gratification. If I pull into a McDonald's drive-thru and hear those awful words, "Pull up and we'll bring your order out to you," I immediately think about changing my order so I don't have to wait. We watch movies where relationships begin and blossom into "happily ever after" in less than ninety minutes. After twenty-nine years of marriage, let me tell you, real relationships take time.

But we want success right now in everything, including our journey with God to overcome our problems. If we're not careful, we'll mistakenly think that once we've chosen to follow God, obey His Word, and connect with a church community, we'll get immediate results. If it doesn't get easy quickly, we might conclude God's way doesn't work.

But this journey with God takes time. Real change doesn't always happen immediately. My walk with God started way back in the summer of 1980. It has taken a long time for me to trust that His way is always better than my way and His timetable for life-change is far wiser than my own.

If you don't like change, join the club. About 70 percent of people are S-type personalities, based on the DISC personality profile. People with this personality fear a lack of security. They want to feel safe, so they stick with what is comfortable or familiar.

Never quit. Those may be the most important words I could ever say to you. As you follow God's direction to face your problems, you will meet resistance. We always do when we try to change.

The universe itself is wired to resist change. One of the Laws of Thermodynamics has to do with entropy—an object in motion tends to stay in motion, but an object at rest tends to stay at rest. If something is going to start moving in a new direction, force must be applied. So it should come as no surprise that if we—who are already mostly resistant to change—are going to change and grow, it's going to take determination to keep moving forward by faith when life gets tough.

But the good news is that we have a God who is stronger than any resistance in the world. He's bigger than our problems, whether they come from other people, within ourselves, or forces of nature. And even better, those of us who've accepted Jesus as our Lord and Savior also have His Spirit living in us. "The one who is in you is greater than the one who is in the world," the Bible tells us (1 John 4:4). If Jesus overcame the power of sin and death, He can definitely handle your problems!

The American church has really hurt Christians by preaching that once you trust Christ, life is going to be great and everything will just work out. The road to a better life will include some problems. That's why you're here, reading this book. To take up your cross and follow Jesus is not an easy thing (Matthew 16:24). If you aren't expecting resistance on the road of following Christ, you won't train for it, and you won't be prepared to fight through when it comes.

I know so many people who have trusted God though facing extreme obstacles. They are an inspiration to me whenever life gets hard. There's one guy here at Legacy Church named Frank who had a difficult childhood. He grew up angry, hateful, and addicted to drugs. Then Frank came to Legacy, and I had the privilege to lead him to Christ. Things started going better for him—he got promoted at work and was making ends meet even during a downturn in the economy.

Then Frank suddenly found himself in a wheelchair. Water had somehow built up in his spine, and he could no longer use his legs. Talk about tough! He could have melted away in self-pity, but he didn't even stop serving at church. His church family didn't give up on him, and he didn't give up on himself or on God. God's grace and love became his strength. Frank tells anyone who will hear that he knows where he came from, and no matter what happens, he won't go back. In his own words, Frank's attitude is: "I just keep moving forward, no looking back. I'm all in, I'm sold out. It's Jesus or nothing at all."

Never Quit

When my son Stevie was in middle school, I coached his basketball team. Our team happened to be the best team in the league and my son was one of our better players. In one game we were playing an inferior team, but we were struggling. For whatever reason, we were not playing well. And I could tell Stevie was getting frustrated with his teammates.

The other team tied the score at the end of the fourth quarter and forced us into overtime. But Stevie already had four fouls; one more and he'd be out of the game. As we started the extra session, I pulled Stevie aside and told him, "Don't give up on your team. Don't quit out there."

Well, pretty soon something happened that frustrated him again. He got angry and intentionally hacked an opposing player for a blatant foul. He was over the limit and out of the game. As he slumped on the bench, I told him, "I'm going to whip your behind when we get home." I didn't actually do it, but I wanted him to get the message loud and clear: Never quit. To this day, he tells that story to teach others the same thing.

In 1 Kings 19, we read the story of another guy who fouled out while serving God. The prophet Elijah, one of the greatest men of faith in all Scripture, had just seen God miraculously send rain after he'd prayed. He had just seen God send fire down from heaven after he'd prayed. He'd just seen the overthrow of hundreds of false prophets. And yet when Elijah's life was threatened by the wicked queen Jezebel, what did he do but run away and hide in a cave.

Now, I'm not saying I would have done any better than he did. The most that's ever happened to me is somebody taking a shot at my truck. So I might have been right there with Elijah had I faced what he faced.

I guess after seeing God do all those mighty works, he thought life was going to get easy. He was unprepared for the adversity that followed God's miracles. So God came to him in a still, small voice and asked him, "What are you doing?" Elijah had apparently rehearsed his script well, because both times God asked, the prophet gave the identical answer:

> "I have been very zealous for the Lord God Almighty. The Israelites have rejected your covenant, torn down your altars, and put your prophets to death with the sword. I am the only one left, and now they are trying to kill me too" (1 Kings 19:10).

Do you know what God told him? God didn't apologize for letting tough times slip past Him into Elijah's life. God didn't step in to change everything immediately so Elijah could live a comfortable life. God responded, not with empathy, but with a call to action. Get back up. Get back in the game. Oh, and by the way, don't believe Satan's lies. You are not alone. I've got seven thousand other people still faithful to me.

I don't know what other teachers and pastors may have told you about the Christian life, but let me shoot straight with you: your life might get darker before it starts getting brighter. That doesn't mean you are off course. In fact, adversity may mean that you are on course with God. You might have to acknowledge that things could get worse before it ever gets better.

Yes, your pain is temporary. But God could have a different definition than you do of *temporary*. It could last for a day, a week, a month, a year, twenty years—I don't know. I do know that "what is seen is temporary" (2 Corinthians 4:8). But God never guarantees the pain will instantly go away.

Lots of church people think we come to Jesus and *boom!* The pain is gone! The beginning of our relationship with God may be like that for a short time, because often God builds up our faith before allowing the enemy to test us. But it's the trying and testing of our faith that causes us to grow and become more like Christ (James 1:2-4).

Whether our reward comes in this life or the next, our job is to just keep serving Jesus. Hebrews 11 lists all these people who lived with great faith but did not receive their reward until they died and went to Heaven. That's tough for some Christians to hear. "You mean I might not get the blessings that I'm thinking I'll get in this life?" The truth is that it might all come in the next life. But really, compared to eternity, this life isn't that long to wait.

Just a Thought:
When the Going Gets Tough

What is your response when things get tough? Do you think, *This must not be the right way*? Do you think God must not want you to go down a path if it gets hard?

The world has taught us to think good things have to feel easy and enjoyable, and whatever feels difficult must be bad for us. When we start going through tough times, we tend to get tunnel vision. The first thought the enemy gives us is *You're the only one.* If we listen, soon we'll start whining, *Why me?* We start focusing inwardly instead of looking up and praying the truth: *OK, God, You knew this was coming. You're not surprised. I'm just going to act on Your Word and keep doing what Your Word says every day, even if I don't feel like it, because my faith is not based on my feelings.*

We have to override our feelings by the power of the Holy Spirit, embrace the truth of God's Word, and determine to live by it no matter what. Just a thought...

Every Day a New Day

Often our problems are not the fault of others but the consequences of our own failures. Those can be even harder to deal with because we know we have no one else to blame. We think, *I messed up and now my life is ruined.* We can fall into the same self-sabotaging thinking patterns, except now we have become our own victim.

Our response in times of personal failure is a test of our faith in God. Failure doesn't mean we're done forever. We can get back up and try again tomorrow, just like lots of people before us. Abraham Lincoln lost several elections before becoming president of the United States. It took Thomas Edison so long to figure out some of his inventions that he famously said, "I haven't failed; I've just found 10,000 ways that won't work."[19] These men saw failure not as a brick wall, but as a catapult to help them learn and do better the next day.

We can't escape the fear of failure; it's part of our nature. But once you recognize it in yourself, you can push past it. Anything that you let stop you from trying again is what will destroy your dreams for a better life.

Remember that our God is the God of another chance. It took me years to understand that every time I failed, God said, "I'm still the God of another chance. I'll never give up on you." If He never gives up on me, I should never give up on myself. I may come up short, but it doesn't mean I can't come up better the next time.

Jesus said, "Everything is possible for one who believes" (Mark 9:23). Do you believe His promises? None of those promises will do you any good if you don't *believe* them. If you believe God is the God of another chance, you'll act on it. You'll get back up when you've failed, accept His forgiveness for your failures, and trust in His unfailing love.

Take people who are trying to kick a bad habit. They may make it two months before they fall. Too often they get caught up in that one moment of failure and forget all about the two months they were clean. If they refuse to let one moment kill two months, they can come back again and do better. The next time they may go three months. Improvement is what we need to focus on if we're thinking like God thinks, because He causes all things to grow (1 Corinthians 3:7). And growth takes time. Even baby steps are pleasing to God when we take them by faith in Him.

Scripture is full of examples of people who got back up after dramatic failures. Peter was one of Jesus's closest friends, but even he denied knowing Him when it mattered. Did Jesus abandon him? No. He helped him back up and empowered him to launch His church. How many times did King David mess up? He committed adultery, lied about it, and then murdered the woman's husband. And this is a man God said was after His own heart! (1 Samuel 13:14). How could God say that about someone who'd done such a horrible thing? I believe it was because he truly repented and refused to let his failure derail him from following after God.

When we accept God's forgiveness for our failures and trust in His unfailing love enough to keep moving forward, we find the supernatural strength to treat every day like a new day. We all falter. We all fail. We all fall. What do we do next? Get back up! Have you seen a little baby who's learning to walk? They hit their head, they bust their rear, they cry, but ten minutes later they're back up and walking again. If only we could be as smart as that baby!

One of the most tragic things I have observed is people who start following God, but then don't finish when the journey gets tough. I've seen men supernaturally delivered from drugs only to watch them return to those same destructive behaviors.

Two guys in particular served in the church for years but continued to struggle with an addiction to cigarettes. They both told me they knew God wanted them to quit. I said, "So quit them." They told me that because God had taken away their desire for drugs, they were waiting for Him to take away the desire for cigarettes as well. I remember telling them that God does do some things supernaturally for us, but He expects us to grow our faith by applying the cleansing Word to our problems. "You need to quit and you need to believe Him to give you the strength," I said. "This one will be a fight, but it's a fight you can win. After all, why would God be dealing with you to do something if He's not going to help you do it?"

I think God wanted them to experience the power of His Word and to learn how to walk through the process of breaking free from the addiction. But apparently they didn't want to go through any pain; they didn't want to fight the strong desires. Both of them continued to struggle, and then slowly they began to fall away in other areas of their lives. In both cases, they ended up back in life situations that were worse than they had before.

Growth is painful. When I started working out a couple of years ago, I learned that lesson, let me tell you. The next day after some workouts it's hard to walk, to sit—man, I'm sore all over! But I know it's good for me. So I don't quit. I keep moving forward.

How God Uses Adversity

We don't truly discover the greatness of God when life is good. We might appreciate His blessings then, but we realize His greatness only when we endure hard times with Him and emerge on the other side. The Bible says that sometimes all we can do is to stand (Ephesians 6:13). That word *stand* essentially means to hang on by the hair of our chinny-chin-chins. It means sometimes all we can do is hang on for dear life.

Maybe all we can say right now is that we're barely making it. Listen, what does it matter if you're *barely* making it if the goal is to make it? So many Christians think we always have to be smiling on this journey, but the truth is sometimes all we can do is hang on by one hand, one finger, or even just a fingernail.

When we reach that desperate place, we need to remind ourselves that God excels at showing up just "at break of day," when the night couldn't possibly get any darker (Psalm 46:5). Too often, we reach the end of our own strength and quit. Adversity is an opportunity for God to show Himself strong on our behalf and demonstrate His unfailing love for us. Trials give God the chance to reveal His power to others through us and prove His promises to us. He is at work within those difficult circumstances to fashion us into the best version of us that we can possibly be. So hang in there, and let Him finish the work He started.

Never Take a Detour

When we trust God enough to keep moving forward, we prove our faith in Him. We show the fruit of our repentance, of our changed heart and mind. That same Thomas Edison who found 10,000 ways *not* to build a lightbulb also said, "Our greatest weakness lies in giving up. The most certain way to succeed is always to try just one more time."[20]

But sometimes when we meet resistance, we try to find an easier way. We think that we can figure out a better way than God's way to reach our destination. So we take a sharp left to find a shortcut—or so we think. But one of the things I love about God is that He doesn't graduate us to the next level of growth until we've learned what He knows we need to learn. Because He knows what is best for us and is working it all for our good, He doesn't let us get away with it.

If we have an issue submitting to authority at work, we may think we'll find a way around the challenge by changing jobs—only to find that we have the same problem in our new job. If we don't face our challenges and keep moving forward by faith, we'll just keep facing the same challenges until we get it right. God loves us too much to let us take a detour around His best for us. When we take a detour, we only hurt ourselves, because here's what we fail to understand: whenever we do eventually choose to follow God's direction, we'll have to return to where we got off course in the first place. We're going to have to face that challenge anyway; we might as well refuse to quit and do it now.

Do you remember the story I told in chapter 4 about my friend Melvin? Do you think it's easy for him to get to church with no legs? No way. Melvin has to piece himself together just to get up each day. What might take most people five minutes takes him half an hour. But he's still here at Legacy Church every Sunday and every Wednesday and plenty of other times. No matter how hard it is for him to get there, he's always smiling and eager to serve. He refuses to quit.

No matter the problems you face right now, you've got to keep moving forward. When you find yourself feeling as if you're crawling on your hands and knees, and everything in you is screaming at you to quit, don't. To use an analogy from my baseball-playing days, you've got to keep practicing well. You may not hit the ball every time. You may even strike out a lot. But if you keep at it, you'll hit enough to make progress. If you stay in motion, God can guide you forward. Often our lives are won or lost by deciding to try one more time, to never give up on the One who never gives up on us.

God's pathway to a better life can be a challenging journey at times. But, like Frank, if we trust God enough to keep moving forward—no matter what—we can see the greatness of the God who is bigger than any problem we might face.

WHAT YOU CAN DO NOW

- When faced with tough times, we often let our fears of what may happen control us. Just the thought of continued pain or discomfort can make us want to quit. Think of a time in your life when you really wanted to quit but didn't. What happened? Were your worst fears realized or were they overrated? What did you learn from that situation?

- As you think about those times when you did not quit in the face of adversity, what were some of the excuses you almost believed? Were they mostly focused outward (on others), inward (on yourself), or upward (on God)? Take a moment to list some excuses you've embraced or nearly embraced in the past and honestly evaluate what they say about where you put your trust.

- What positive outcomes came from your refusing to quit? List the rewards you experienced from patiently enduring a challenge or facing adversity once you persevered to the other side.

- Try to remember a time when *someone else* didn't give up *on you* or didn't quit *for you*. Was it a parent? A teacher? A friend? If you can't think of anyone, you're not thinking hard enough, because God should be at the top of that list. If you've never done so, take a moment now to drop that person a note or email and thank them for standing with you and inspiring you to never quit.

- People who are successful at anything in life don't quit. And when they fail, they get back up and try again. If you think you may have already quit or failed, what would it take for you to try again? Seek out someone you can trust with your dream of beginning again, someone who will encourage you and hold you accountable for going after it. Ask them to help you be successful.

12

CELEBRATE EACH
AND EVERY VICTORY

Have you ever witnessed babies taking their first steps? When they first learn to stand, they hang on for dear life. Then one day they decide to take a step on their own; they take one wobbly step and fall right down. But what do we do? We clap and cheer! We record the moment on video. We pass it around on Facebook. We go crazy and celebrate because they took one little step. Encouraged by our response, the next day they'll try again, take two steps, and then fall down again—but we'll celebrate the two steps. We celebrate each and every victory with them no matter how small.

Why wouldn't we do the same for ourselves on this journey with God? Why wouldn't we celebrate each and every victory as we face and overcome spiritual obstacles? I don't know about you, but I need all the encouragement I can get! The Bible says we should celebrate even the very day that God has made, so certainly His work in our lives is worth a party or two (Psalm 118:24).

I introduced you to Melvin earlier. He serves so much you can't go to Legacy Church for any length of time and not know who he is. He's also pretty easy to pick out because of his prosthetic legs. You would be hard-pressed to find someone facing bigger problems, but

Melvin radiates joy and gratitude. He's just thankful to be used by God as a vessel to help others. Melvin knows what it takes to conquer mountains—and to celebrate when he succeeds.

I'll never forget the day I saw Melvin walk again. He came to the church and said, "Pastor Steve, the doctor said I could never do this." Then he stood up on those two prosthetic legs and took a step. He couldn't balance very well, but you should've seen the smile on his face as he stood and walked away from his wheelchair. And you should have heard his family hollering and whooping it up as he took that first step! One huge reason Melvin can stay joyful is that he and his family celebrate every single victory.

I have found that it's often the little victories—and what we do with them—that can make the difference for our long-term success. I love how the Western novelist Louis L'Amour put it: "Victory is won not in miles but in inches. Win a little now, hold your ground, and later, win a little more."[21]

Sounds like a plan to me.

Choose Your Cheering Section

Our culture is quick to remind us of the reasons we cannot succeed. We're not qualified. We're not good-looking. We're not rich enough. We're not educated enough. We're surrounded by negative voices—the world, the flesh, and the devil—that seek to pull us down to their level. Your enemies would like nothing better than for you to sink back into thinking and living as if there is no hope for a better tomorrow.

Those who are influenced by the world want you to think the same way they do, and they do everything in their power to keep you from changing. When you begin to live, act, and think differently, many of your old friends won't be comfortable with you anymore. They just won't "get" you. And they certainly won't celebrate victories in your walk with Christ. They'll try to bring you back to a place where they are comfortable with you.

If you tell them you've quit drinking, they'll want to buy you drinks. If you've stopped lying at your job, they'll pressure you to bend the rules. When you start going to church, they'll invite you to go places on Sunday so you'll miss the service. It's not that they are necessarily trying to destroy you, but they want to feel better about themselves by pulling you back down.

Even a culture so obsessed with becoming rich and famous shows its true colors when someone actually works hard and achieves financial success. Suddenly, the tables turn and the airwaves fill with envy and demands that the wealth be shared with others. For all the talk about success, most people are envious of the success of others. They think successful people don't deserve it or they must be cheating, as if there's only so much to go around.

So if your life starts to improve, some people try to pull you off course instead of celebrating your success. If you say, "I'm changing the way I talk, the way I treat my spouse, and how I lead my children," you'd think they would be happy for you. Instead, they may criticize you, call you weird, or ridicule your faith in God. Your positive behavior exposes their shortcomings and brings their relationship with God into focus, and they don't like what they see. So they self-sabotage themselves by trying to sabotage you.

If you want people to celebrate your successes on this journey to a better life, you must relocate your relationships. That's why finding the right church community is so important. We must find people we can celebrate with if we are going to push back all the negative voices that surround us. We need to surround ourselves with people who will genuinely be happy for our success. We need people who will say, "Good job, that's awesome!" instead of "Why would you want to do that?" or "I liked you better before." If we are going to succeed over time, we need to celebrate each and every victory, not wait until we achieve our ultimate goal. Like Melvin, we must learn to celebrate every step we take.

What Gets Rewarded Gets Repeated

It's a basic principle of parenting, of leading, of teaching, even of training dogs. Whatever behavior you reward is the behavior you will see repeated. That's how we human beings work. We respond to rewards. When we celebrate success, no matter how small it may seem, we reinforce in our minds the importance of continuing down this pathway to a better life.

When you celebrate each victory, you train yourself to succeed again the next time. You develop a champion mentality. When a team is playing in a championship game for the first time, a coach will tell his players, "Play like you've been here before." It's the victory mindset that fuels their determination to win the game.

I'm leading a bigger church today than I ever imagined. If you ask me what I'm doing, I'll tell you: I don't know! Every day I'm learning. I've never been here before. But I can look back at past levels where I had never been before and see that God gave me just what I needed to succeed. He rewarded me for my faithfulness in those times, and so I am quick to trust Him today when I think I'm in over my head. Now I have a foundation to build on and the confidence that He'll continue to help me succeed. Every victory I've had inspires me to stick with God when the journey gets tough.

Sometimes we may feel awkward about celebrating the good that God has done in our lives. We're afraid it might sound as if we are bragging. Although I don't know your heart motivation, I know it's OK to feel good when you accomplish something; it's OK to be confident. The only people who don't like confident people are those who are not confident in themselves. Confidence is attractive; pride is not.

In Christ, you are a new creature empowered by the Holy Spirit, able to do what you once thought impossible. If that doesn't sound like a reason to be confident, I don't know what would be. So don't ever allow yourself to be ashamed of what God does in your life. People need to see our good works and the rewards that come with them, so they will glorify our Father in heaven (Matthew 5:16).

God promises abundant rewards for those who continue to walk with Him faithfully. Jesus told His disciples to ask Him for things. He said, "Until now you have not asked for anything in my name. Ask and you will receive." And why were they supposed to ask? So their "joy will be complete" (John 16:24). God wants us to experience joy as we walk with Him. As we do, we'll be eager to trust more, walk closer, and prepare for a party in eternity that is out of this world.

The Power of the Positive

The Disney/Pixar film *Monsters, Inc.* made us laugh at the thought of running an entire city on the energy derived from children's screams—their negative energy. Yet it was when the monsters discovered the positive energy of laughter that their capacity increased exponentially. So it is with us. When we focus on the power of the positive in our words, deeds, and thoughts, we position ourselves to walk with unprecedented faith in God's power to do something truly great through us.

Here are five tips to help you focus on the positive so you can celebrate your own success and that of others:

1. Make a list of all the things you've achieved in your life. It's OK to be proud of what you've accomplished as long

as it doesn't cause you to rob God of His glory. Instead of being your own worst critic, try seeing yourself as your own best. When we do our best to look at our lives objectively, it's easier to recognize our successes instead of simply focusing on our shortcomings.

2. Keep a journal about your successes and failures and what you learned from them. Even when we fail, we should not fail to learn something from it.

3. When you make a to-do list, make a "done list" to go with it. It's far more encouraging to see what you've checked off instead of what's left to do. We often don't realize how much we've accomplished until we can visually see the progress we've made.

4. When you reach a goal, treat yourself. Go out to eat (you can invite others to join in if you want). Buy something you've been wanting if it's in your budget. It doesn't have to cost money, of course, but find a way to celebrate. Remember, what gets rewarded gets repeated.

5. Make friendships with others who share similar goals and aspirations. Help each other to celebrate success. Encourage others to reach their goals and cheer them on!

Your Personal Definition of Success

When I say victory or success, I don't mean the kind of success the world holds up—money, popularity, power, fame, and pleasure. I'm not talking about having mansions and jets. That may be God's best for you, I don't know. But I've seen a lot more people destroyed by personal wealth than helped by it.

We need to define success by God's standards. Success is just doing what God wants us to do—and that's a little different for everyone. Sure, we're all given the same set of commandants and expectations about the big things in life. God gives clear-cut wisdom we're to follow in His Word on a lot of things. But He also leaves a lot unsaid, so we can trust Him as we walk out our faith each and every day.

For Melvin, success was just being able to stand and take a step. For my wife, it means a happy marriage in which she knows her husband would never abuse her. For Michelangelo, it means breaking free of a destructive lifestyle and finding physical healing. For so many children, success would mean a home that's peaceful instead of full of turmoil.

What may not be important to you might be huge to somebody else. To somebody who's making $20,000 a year, getting a job making $30,000 is the epitome of success. They'd think they had reached the stars. For others it would mean making $100,000. For others, the money may not be worth anything. I've met people who are rich, but they have just as many health problems as they have bank accounts. And they would give it all away just to be healthy.

For you it may mean personal healing from a relationship torn apart long ago. For your neighbor, success may mean starting his or her own business. Some of my most significant successes are ones no one else ever knew about—changes in my own thinking. In other words, there is no one-size-fits-all victory in Christ.

We cannot let someone else define our success or compare our success to another. God has a unique plan for each of us. Wallowing in self-pity because you want someone else's life is bad enough, but living to achieve someone else's version of success can be even more frustrating because it's not the path God has for you. If I tried to live your life, I'd be miserable. If you tried to live mine, you'd likely burn this book in frustration. But that's OK, because God leads each of us on a different path to find joy.

Joy is what gives us the power to continue with God. The Bible says the joy of the Lord is our strength (Nehemiah 8:10). It doesn't say that joy itself is our strength. It is the joy *of the Lord*; it's what brings God joy. Here's how I paraphrase it: Whatever brings God joy makes you strong. Whenever I follow God in His ways, I bring Him joy, and in doing so, I become strong. So my success should not be about my joy but about His joy. The pursuit of what gives God joy is what sustains us when everything else goes crazy. When we're tempted to panic when stuff doesn't go right, it's the joy of the Lord that gives us hope and whispers, "Everything's going to be OK."

Pitfalls to Avoid When Defining Your Success

Your definition of success must be based on God's definition. It will be personal to you, but you can't just make up what you want to get out of life. Your definition of success must never contradict what God's Word says. And you can't define success by what other people think it should be for you. They can give input—perhaps even valuable advice—but the final say has to be God's will and design for you.

Here are some other common pitfalls to avoid when defining what success looks like in your life:

- Success does not mean that life will be trouble free.
- Success does not mean that you have arrived and can now stop growing.
- Success does not mean that you now know everything.
- Success does not mean that you are better than someone else.

- Success in one area of life doesn't mean you can stop moving forward in others.

- Success does not mean that you don't need input from others.

- Success does not mean you can stop playing the hand you've been dealt.

- Success does not give you permission to coast or settle for less than God's best.

Just a Thought:
The Deception of Envy

Do you envy other people's success? Here is something to think about: whatever you begrudge in someone else's life, you will never have in your life. When you complain that someone else doesn't deserve the blessing God has given them, it's as if you are saying to God, "That car is too nice, that house is too big, or that job pays too much money— I don't ever want to have those things." Why would you want them if, in fact, they are so bad?

You see, covetousness is deceptive. We think we desire a better life, but really we're just feeding a victim mentality. Instead of being jealous, rejoice with those who overcome an obstacle, get a raise, or receive physical blessings. Our celebration frees God to bring some of our own desires to fruition in our lives. Watching others receive a blessing is a proving time—we prove our faith while we wait. When we trust God and rejoice with others one day at a time, we'll soon look back and see how far we've come and hear others rejoicing over our own growth. Just a thought...

Celebrate the Success of Others

We not only need to surround ourselves with people who will help us celebrate God's goodness in our own lives—we must be that person for others too. The good news is that rejoicing with others can be a natural habit to develop. For example, when we receive a compliment, we automatically look for some way to give a compliment in return. If I rejoice with you, you will be more likely to rejoice with me.

And there is so much to celebrate if we're willing to see what God is doing around us. Have you ever listened to someone's testimony of how Christ changed their life and thought, *That is amazing! I would have never guessed, because who they are today is completely different?* I hear people's stories all the time, yet I never cease to be amazed by what God can do with a life when that person absorbs His Word and applies it.

I met a young lady who was once a drug dealer, a rebel, and in prison, but when she got out, God changed her life. The whole time she was telling me her story, I was thinking that if she hadn't told me, I would have never believed it. The young woman in front of me didn't look at all like a drug dealer or ex-convict. God had turned her life around—a complete 180! I celebrated both God's work in her and her own effort to get there, because she had to endure a lot to make that kind of life-change.

Another guy I know was once part of a notorious motorcycle gang and lived that stereotypical lifestyle—rugged, tough, and mean. He wasn't faithful to his wife, but he actually came to church to see if she was cheating on him. When he didn't find her with someone else, he sat down and listened to the sermon. By the end of the service, he'd given his life to the Lord. If you were to meet him today, you would never believe who he used to be. He's a wonderful guy, faithful, generous, and loves God from the inside out. I love celebrating stories like his, because only God could do that.

If I become envious or begrudge another's success, I can't celebrate with them. I only see what I don't have. True faith in God produces godliness with contentment, a combination that the biblical writer Timothy says produces "great gain" (1 Timothy 6:6). It frees us to celebrate success wherever we might find it without envy or guilt.

Sadly, when God blesses some Christians, they act ashamed out of fear of what others might think. I came out of my office one day and saw a lady who attends our church driving a new car. I had never seen her drive it before, so I said, "Nice car." That's all I said. It was a nice car, after all. But she immediately began telling me how it was only a used car and that she and her husband got it at a terrific price. I stopped her and said, "You don't have to make excuses for driving such a nice car. I'm excited for you. You work hard and are faithful to God, and He's blessing you." Without even realizing it, she was belittling her own blessing. She assumed that I would not rejoice with her. Unfortunately, she may have thought that because she'd heard that response within the church before.

Have you ever genuinely rejoiced to share a blessing and were told, "Pride comes before a fall" or "God gives grace only to the humble"? The intention behind these expressions might sound pious, but in that setting, they're wrong and misguided. The Bible says to rejoice with those who rejoice and to weep with those who weep (Romans 12:15). Do you know why we find that crying part easier to do? Because we're OK with someone doing worse than we are, but we don't like it when they do better. We become envious of their success. Rather than falling for envy, we need to renew our minds and just obey what the Word says—celebrate the success of others. And just see if our celebration of their success doesn't move us to pursue some new victories of our own.

WHAT YOU CAN DO NOW

Take this mini-assessment of how you view your own success and the success of others:

How do you respond when you reach an important goal or have success in your life?

- Do you feel humble and thankful or do you think that it was the least you deserved?

- Do you celebrate your success or minimize it? Like my friend with the Mercedes, do you make excuses to others that diminish God's blessings to you?

- Do you tell yourself you did a good job, or do you believe that you don't deserve compliments when you succeed? What comes to mind in those moments? Do you replay past mistakes or just chalk it up to dumb luck?

- Do you still compare yourself to others when you achieve a victory?

- Do you share the good news of God's victories in your life or hide it?

How do you respond when others succeed?

- Do you celebrate with others' successes or think, *That should have been me*?

- Do you belittle the success of others or find reasons why it isn't that impressive? Do you say things like, "He only got the raise because he butters up the boss" or "If I'd had that opportunity, I would have done even better"?

- Do you give credit for others' good work or try to take credit for yourself?

- What do you say when someone compliments you for something someone else did or that you did together as a team?

- What do you say to the person who succeeds? Do you warn them about pride when they celebrate God's blessing?

13

MY PRAYER
FOR YOU

As I said when our journey began, I don't know the details of whatever problems you face. What you've read about a pathway to a better life is based on my personal journey and the Word of God. Some of it has been amazing, some not so much. As the Author and Finisher of my faith, I believe Jesus has led me the entire way. I have been hurt, disappointed, angry, and discouraged at times. I have also been blessed, joyful, and excited. Either way, God is still God. He is good when everything is going my way, and He is good when things don't seem to be going my way.

Those of us who serve Him are like cats—no matter what life's circumstances may throw our way, we will always land on our feet. This journey has taught me to trust God no matter what the circumstances and to believe that, whatever goes on in my life, it will always work out for my good and His glory. So there are no wasted moments as we serve God. Wasted opportunities, maybe. But not wasted moments.

My hope is that as you have read this book, you've begun to put into practice the principles of God's Word so you can experience significant life-change—long-lasting change that causes not only you but those around you to live a better life. We will all have problems. It's how we respond to them, the attitudes we embrace when going through them, that will make the difference.

There is always hope. May that thought resonate deep within you. Know that there is never a reason to quit or give up on your life. A life in service for God is not always easy, nor does He promise it will be. But it is always a fulfilling life with no regrets. I have never heard anyone—after serving the Lord their entire life—say, "I regret having served God." I've seen people regret not serving the Lord, but not the one who recognizes His greatness and experiences His strength and power.

So I've laid out some of my hurt and pain in these pages, some of my failures and successes, and how I've learned by God's grace to be better, do better, and live a better life. I really do have a wonderful life and God gets all the credit. But it didn't come without a cost. It's come at a cost of denying myself and being willing to deal with stuff that hasn't always been easy to face. It's been well worth it. I have a long way to go, but I know I won't be alone.

As you have read this book, I pray God has spoken to you to make your steps clear. I believe no one really wants to be a victim or feel helpless. None of us have to be if we are willing to take God's Word and apply it each and every day. If we want to avoid an emotional life, we must develop a healthy devotional life. And the fastest way to grow is to never take a detour. We must stay on the straight and narrow, realize God's Word works, and know that we have work to do, as well.

The journey starts now, not tomorrow. It begins when you decide to confront the things in your life that cause you to play the victim card and self-sabotage your future. God has given us everything we need to overcome in this life, to be truly free from what ails us. If only we will believe. If only we will judge ourselves. If only we will cry out to God for His help. The person the Son sets free is free indeed (John 8:36)!

Let's be willing to truly choose a new direction, repent (change our minds, attitudes, actions), and receive God's forgiveness. Let's have the courage to push past our fears and allow God by His Holy Spirit to do spiritual surgery in our hearts and minds.

I've shared many stories of people who have gone through some tough stuff and yet overcome. It's one day at a time for all of us; that's all we can do. It should comfort us to know that God will never reject us or abandon us on this journey (Hebrews 13:5). It takes faith to trust that God is there to help us keep playing the hand we've been dealt. We may not like those cards, but we need to play them and see if we don't begin to get better cards as we move forward, allowing the Holy Spirit to lead and guide us into all truth. The Word of God is what will help us. If God's Word says it, then believe it.

Paul prayed this prayer for the Christians at Ephesus. I pray it for you now:

> [For I always pray to] the God of our Lord Jesus Christ, the Father of glory, that He may grant you a spirit of wisdom and revelation [of insight into mysteries and secrets] in the [deep and intimate] knowledge of Him, by having the eyes of your heart flooded with light, so that you can know *and* understand the hope to which He has called you, and how rich is His glorious inheritance in the saints (His set-apart ones), and [so that you can know and understand] what is the immeasurable *and* unlimited *and* surpassing greatness of His power in *and* for us who believe, as demonstrated in the working of His mighty strength, which He exerted in Christ when He raised Him from the dead and seated Him at

His [own] right hand in the heavenly [places], far above all rule and authority and power and dominion and every name that is named [above every title that can be conferred], not only in this age *and* in this world, but also in the age *and* the world which are to come (Ephesians 1:17-21 AMP).

So no more blaming! Take responsibility for how you will respond to the problems you face and watch what God does. As you follow God's Word, don't quit when you meet resistance. Trust God enough to keep moving forward. Be committed to grow in order to work out your problems. And no matter how big your problems may appear to you, know that God is always bigger.

If you are willing to follow God's wisdom and walk in His proven pathway, you will become the best version of you that you could possibly be. God has whatever you need for whatever you face— and He's offering it to you.

NOTES

1. "Houston, We've Had a Problem," James A. Lovell, *Apollo Expeditions to the Moon*, http://history.nasa.gov/SP-350/ch-13-1.html.

2. "Morbidity and Mortality Weekly Report," *Centers for Disease Control and Prevention*, October 1, 2010, www.cdc.gov/mmwr/preview/mmwrhtml/mm5938a2.htm.

3. "Suicide and Self-Inflicted Injury," *Centers for Disease Control and Prevention*, www.cdc .gov/nchs/fastats/suicide.htm.

4. "Trends and Statistics," *National Institute on Drug Abuse*, www.drugabuse.gov/ related-topics/trends-statistics.

5. "Stats," *XXXchurch*, www.xxxchurch.com/extras/pornographystatistics.html.

6. "Public Sees Religion's Influence Waning," *Pew Research Center*, September 22, 2014, www.pewforum.org/2014/09/22/public-sees-religions-influence-waning-2/.

7. "Religion Among the Millennials," *Pew Research Center*, February 17, 2010, www.pew forum.org/2010/02/17/religion-among-the-millennials/.

8. Adapted from "How to Know You've Given Up Trying to Be Amazing," *Dan Waldschmidt* (blog), http://danwaldschmidt.com/2012/04/attitude/how-to-know-youve-given-up-trying-to-be-amazing.

9. A January 2014 survey from the Pew Forum demonstrated that

   - 50 percent of people surveyed said that circumstances beyond an individual's control rather than hard work were the primary cause of wealth or poverty;

   - 38 percent of the people surveyed said that work and determination are no guarantee of success for most people;

   - 53 percent of people surveyed said that the government should do a lot to reduce poverty;

- 43 percent said that the government should do a lot to reduce the gap between the rich and everyone else (wealth redistribution);
- 60 percent said that the economic system in the United States favors the wealthy.

"Most See Inequality Growing, But Partisans Differ Over Solutions," *Pew Research Center*, January 23, 2014 (www.people-press.org/2014/01/23/most-see-inequality-growing-but-partisans-differ-over-solutions/).

10. "William Wilberforce Quotes," *Brainy Quote*, www.brainyquote.com/quotes/authors/w/william_wilberforce.html.

11. "Albert Einstein Quotes," *Brainy Quote*, www.brainyquote.com/quotes/authors/a/albert_einstein.html.

12. D.A. Carson, *For the Love of God*, vol. 2 (Wheaton, IL: Crossway Books, 1999).

13. Tom Moon, "Are We Hardwired for Unhappiness?: 1. The Brain's Negative Bias," *Tom Moon, MFT* (blog), http://tommoon.net/articles/are_we_hardwired-1.html.

14. "Negative Thinking: Necessary for Survival; Limiting for Success," *MyBrainSolutions*, August 14, 2013, www.mybrainsolutions.com/library/2013/08/negative-thinking-necessary-for-safety-limiting-for-success/.

15. Raj Raghunathan, "How Negative Is Your 'Mental Chatter'?" *Psychology Today*, October 10, 2013, www.psychologytoday.com/blog/sapient-nature/201310/how-negative-is-your-mental-chatter.

16. "Henry David Thoreau Quotes," *Brainy Quote*, www.brainyquote.com/quotes/authors/h/henry_david_thoreau.html.

17. This quote is widely attributed to Johann Wolfgang von Goethe, but it is more likely from William H. Murray in *The Scottish Himalaya Expedition*, http://en.wikiquote.org/wiki/W._H._Murray.

18. Randy Alcorn, *The Law of Rewards* (Carol Stream, IL: Tyndale House, 2003), 12.

19. "Thomas A. Edison Quotes," *Goodreads*, www.goodreads.com/author/quotes/3091287.Thomas_A_Edison.

20. "Thomas A. Edison Quotes," *Brainy Quote*, www.brainyquote.com/quotes/quotes/t/thomasaed149049.html.

21. "Victory Quotes," November 3, 2006, *Quotes and Phrases*, http://quotesnphrases.blogspot.com/2006/11/victory-quotes.html.

ABOUT THE AUTHOR

Steve Smothermon is senior pastor of Legacy Church, a large and growing church in Albuquerque, New Mexico (www.legacychurchnm.com). He earned a bachelor of theological studies degree from Vision International University and is the author of *Large Large Living in a Small Small World*. Steve and his wife, Cynthia, have been married for almost 30 years and are the proud parents of three children and a growing number of grandchildren.

To learn more about Harvest House books and
to read sample chapters, visit our website:

www.harvesthousepublishers.com

HARVEST HOUSE PUBLISHERS
EUGENE, OREGON